THE SPRING WIND

THE SPRING WIND

by Gladis DePree

Drawings by James N. Howard

HARPER & ROW, PUBLISHERS
NEW YORK, EVANSTON, AND LONDON

FIRST EDITION

LIBRARY OF CONGRESS
CATALOG CARD NUMBER: 70–109064

To our children
Marita, Michael, Deidra, and Christopher
Who have been the best part of everything

Contents

Acknowledgments

Chapters 9 and 10 originally appeared as short stories in *The Church Herald* under the titles "Born in a Market" (December 20, 1968) and "Why Did You Come to Our Village?" (February 7, 1969) respectively. Louis H. Benes, editor of *The Church Herald*, has kindly granted permission for their inclusion here.

My deepest gratitude is to Dr. and Mrs. Norman Vincent Peale, whose interest in our efforts and work in Hong Kong has been a source of encouragement and inspiration.

I am indebted to Myron Boardman of the Foundation for Christian Living in Pawling, New York, for his advice and direction.

My sincere thanks to Miss Eleanor Jordan of Harper & Row for her keen insight as editor of this book.

G.D.P.

A Note to the Reader

This story takes place in Hong Kong, for many of us a mysterious faraway city. The names of the streets are strange. The people have daily rice instead of daily bread, and the language sounds as though someone were singing a tune.

But you could take this story, change the names, fill in your own local color, and it would be just as exciting. The world is shrinking, and we no longer have faraway stories and nearby stories. We only have stories of people, and of their relationship to each other as human or inhuman beings.

The Spring Wind is loosely set in time and place. Hopefully, after you have read this story the pieces of its pattern will fall apart in your hands, daring you to reassemble them in the frame of your own experience.

This is our frame, Gordon's and mine, and these were our experiences. We invite you to read them for what they may mean to you.

Gladis DePree

THE SPRING WIND

1   Finding the Questions

At ten o'clock the Hong Kong summer morning was already hot and humid. I climbed the stairs on the sixth floor of the Old China Language School and walked out onto the quietness of the roof. Even here the sun beat down blindingly.

The quietness of the roof, like the heat, was comparative. It was not silent, but of a different intensity from the buzz of voices in the hallway below.

I walked to the edge of the enclosure and looked down over the neighborhood. In every direction tall buildings were jammed together, making the heat of the pavement seem denser and more unbearable. The odor of garlic and dried fish and crowded humanity wafted up to the rooftop, mixed with the rhythmic chanting of multiplication tables in Cantonese from the primary school next door. Somewhere, from one of the windows in one of the buildings, a woman's voice called and a child answered. Horns tooted in the street below, and a jet roared overhead. There were sounds, but they were external sounds, other people's sounds, not disturbing sounds like the conversations downstairs.

I leaned on the rough cement railing and looked out across the rooftops. The buildings melted into the blue of the sea, then took form again across the harbor on Hong Kong Island. It had been on a torrid sticky morning such as this, three years ago, that we had gone to Check Wan market on the south side of the island. Many times I had tried to forget that incident, to pretend it had never happened . . .

We had gone that day, Gordon and I, to the village to paint. We parked our mini-car across from a vegetable stall, surrounded by produce baskets, baby chicks, and small children. The old woman in the stall was intriguing, in her baggy black trousers and silver hair done up in a knot. She worked on, oblivious of being sketched. She weighed out a handful of *choi sum* in the twine-and-metal scale and wound it with string for her customer, a young woman with a baby strapped on her back.

Gordon left the car and walked down past the rice-wine factory to the sea where the fishing boats bobbed in the blue water. I sketched quickly, anxious to include the woman with the baby before she too disappeared down the narrow winding road.

Suddenly, there was a face at the car window. I looked up and saw a pair of laughing dark eyes shadowed by a shock of wiry black hair. A young boy of about twelve stood smiling shyly, as though he wished he could speak but knew I would not understand.

The old woman glanced toward the car. She uneasily smoothed her silver hair back and straightened the white apron that hung over her loose trousers, then abruptly, as though she had resolved some problem, she called out in a shrill, throaty voice . . .

"Ah Sung-a!"

The boy raised his head and ran to her, scattering the chickens as he went. A delivery truck lumbered between us, taking up the whole roadway, and for a moment I could not see him. Then I saw them both, the old woman and the boy, coming toward the car.

I held up the sketch for her to see, expecting her to be pleased. Instead, she smiled politely and held out her hand for money. A sensation of annoyance and embarrassment gripped me. There was no money, except in Gordon's pocket down the street, and furthermore, I had not asked her to pose. As far as I was concerned, she and the cucumbers and spring onions were all a part of the scenery.

I turned my empty palms up, and shook my head negatively.

She smiled, bowed slightly, and shook her head in the opposite direction.

I glanced anxiously up and down the street, but Gordon was nowhere in sight. There was no way to explain. In desperation I rolled up the window and turned the other way.

I could hear her muttering outside the window. A young man came, then several men. They seemed to come from the baskets and out of the spaces between the stalls. There were a dozen . . . A crowd began collecting, and there was the hum of angry voices. A man rapped sharply on the window, and I locked the door, fear pounding through me like a leaden hammer . . .

Then as though nothing had happened, Gordon reappeared. He walked through the crowd, smiling slightly, got into the car, and we were off without further incident. For a moment I thought I could have imagined it all.

But that afternoon as I worked on the painting, the spirit of it was gone. In place of the canvas before me there were faces . . . The friendly face of a boy, eager, curious, open, and the dark scowling face of a boy on the edge of a crowd, angry, resentful, scornful. They were the same face with different expressions. In fact, the face itself had faded and only the expressions remained, remained just below the surface ready to spring up and take the form of other faces, a procession of faces. One of the faces was mine, twisted with fear, locking a door . . .

I set the picture aside, unable to concentrate on cucumbers and baggy trousers. What meaning was there in painting the surface of things when one did not understand the conflicts that lay beneath them? *Must men live like this? Were mistrust and fear between people a necessary part of existence? Was there no way of smashing out of these hideous prisons, of living together as persons who dared to look one another in the face as human beings, and not as kinds of people?*

Perhaps the question was even more perplexing this morning than it had been three years ago. Then we had been Americans working with American military overseas. We had been outsiders in the Chinese world. But now we had come back at the invitation of the leaders of the Chinese Church to work with them in their city. It was our concern that we understand the situation as insiders, not as those who searched for the sensational and different, but as those who looked for our common oneness as persons in a fast-shrinking world. Sometimes the whole situation seemed overwhelming.

I went downstairs to look for Gordon. The hallway was still buzzing with languages and nuances. Two Indian Army officers were talking to a Japanese girl in Mandarin. A Catholic sister was trading Peanuts jokes with a Baptist missionary. A doctor was discussing worm remedies with an orphanage matron. A man from the consulate was talking about private boats with a social worker.

"Where do you live now?" said an unidentified voice behind me.

"We're still in the hotel looking for a place," another voice answered. "When we came we had hoped to live right in the city, you know, up over a shop in some busy area, but I think we've changed our minds. It seems that people have tried it, and it hasn't worked."

"Why not?"

"Well, we have children, you know, and I suppose the mission house would be a bit more sensible. It's in a quiet area, away from things a bit. My wife says if we live in a crowded community there's no place for the children to play except on the dirty street . . . and I do feel I have a certain obligation to provide for my family."

"Of course, of course. But what about the Chinese children who play on the street?"

"I don't know how they survive. Must have a built-in immunity to germs. But I think you can get bogged down in this sort of thing, too. I figure the most important part of being here is not where you live, but whether or not you're effective in your job, and frankly I couldn't think or work effectively with Cantonese music in one ear and MaJong tiles clicking in the other. I simply can't work in all that noise and confusion."

"What work will you be doing?"

"Well . . . that's the question. I'm not sure yet."

I picked up a cup and looked for some hot water. It was in a thermos with a pungent-smelling cork. Even on the hottest days we drank hot water. For a moment I wondered why nobody ever brought ice water, and then I thought of all the trouble involved in boiling water, chilling it, freezing ice . . . One cup of hot water with a little instant coffee went a long way.

". . . I can't see why people get so perturbed about identifying with the culture," a woman was saying. "To me, the whole thing is ridiculous. Why shouldn't I be myself? We have our ways, and they have theirs. Frankly, with my figure, I look terrible in a *choengsam*, and with my digestion I'd soon perish on rice and noodles. Government and business people make no bones about living comfortably . . . Why should they expect us to be any different?"

I could see Gordon now at the end of the hallway talking to Father Schaperelli. It was a new experience for us to converse with sisters and priests, and we were fascinated by them. I watched them standing together, the short muscular Father and Gordon with his long cowboy legs, and wondered what the world was coming to.

The Father was talking, and Gordon, as usual, was listening.

"It's too bad you missed that meeting," he was saying. "We

almost got down to something valid. You know, sometimes you have these questions, and no one dares ask them, and you pussyfoot around all night talking over things no one gives a hoot about . . . I'm telling you, I get hungry for some real confrontation! So when this guy asked for questions from the floor, I let him have it. I stood up and said, 'Mr. Chairman, I have a question I'd like to throw out for discussion tonight. Since we're not here to save the heathen from hell anymore, why are we here?' "

"What did he say?" Gordon asked.

"The chairman didn't have a chance to say anything. This fellow behind me popped up and said, 'Now wait a minute, Schaperelli! I believe you've started from an assumption that many of us do not have. I don't know what *you're* doing here, but there are still many of us who consider the Chinese heathen idol-worshipers who need to be saved from hell . . .' "

The class bell sounded like a fire alarm through the hallway, blotting out the voices. Gordon turned and held out his hand, and I took it, grateful for his reassuring grip in all this confusion.

Perhaps it was the smallness of the classrooms, or the heat, or the unbearable humiliation of grown men and women being reduced to babbling like infants . . . Whatever it was made nerves jangle and tempers flare. In our room there were nine adults, most of them classified as missionaries. The majority were Americans. Our most frequent teacher was Mrs. Lee, a tiny Chinese woman with perceptive black eyes that could make a six-foot man shrivel. She was at once a dainty woman and a driver, and what she could not accomplish with one force, she could with the other. In the classroom, she was complete master . . .

"Mr. Jones, read the second sound in the seven tones."

"*Ba, ba, ba, ba, ba, ba, bah.*"

"Your high-falling isn't right. Say it like an exclamation."

"*Bah?*"

"Exclamation!"

"*Bah!*" he said with feeling.

As the summer became hotter the lessons became more difficult. It was amusing to hear Cantonese spoken with Texan accents, Michigan accents, South Carolina accents. Particularly difficult for me was the word "book." Every time it appeared, Mrs. Lee seemed to point to me, and I would have a feeling of panic. *Book . . . how can I say book . . . I'm totally illiterate in this culture . . . I can't even pick up a kindergarten book and read it . . . I'm never going to get this language . . . What if Gordon learns it and I don't . . . ? What if I simply can't?*

The terrible realization of being illiterate, and the sense of inferiority it created, made my mind a blank. And I refused to say "book" or even to think about it.

It was strange how the fear of failure affected us. Our fears seemed to be dictated by our expectations, and whatever we hoped to do most, we had the greatest fear of not doing. There was the day when we began to study Chinese family relationships on a simple level.

"Relationships are important to us," said Mrs. Lee. "In Chinese culture, one's whole position in life is influenced by his place in the family structure. The elder brother has a great responsibility to the younger; the younger brother must show due respect to the elder. Mr. Porter, do you recall the word for elder brother?"

Porter was doodling an elaborate cross in his notebook and did not respond. He had been doing poorly in class and was becoming tense and moody.

Mrs. Lee tapped the book with her pencil.

"Mr. Porter?"

He looked up slowly.

"Mr. Porter, since this lesson is obviously not very interesting to you, would you care to answer this question for me? How many brothers do you have?"

We waited motionlessly, feeling the loaded import of the question.

"I have—"

"Use Cantonese, please."

"*Naw—*"

"More of an *ng* sound, like the end of running."

"*Ngaw yeow—*"

"*Yauh*, please, not like a cat's meow."

"*Ngaw yeow sam—*"

"*Saam!* Make it a high falling tone."

Porter's breath was coming in short gasps. His face was red, and his fists were clenched to hide his trembling fingers. He looked fiercely at the woman standing in front of the room humiliating him.

"I—" he choked. "You—you're wasting my time! I've been sitting here for weeks, and what can I say? Nothing right, not even one word! And you stand there wasting a whole class period on Chinese family relationships. Why should I care about a culture that's heathen and evil at the root? I came here to teach people, not to learn their ways. I don't care how many brothers a man has! All I ask you to teach me are the words I need to ask a man about his relationship to God. That's the only relationship I'm concerned about!"

The tiny woman's eyes were black pools of amused anger.

"Does anyone in the classroom share Mr. Porter's opinion?" she asked tersely.

It was so quiet I could hear my heart thundering in my ears. *Who of us had not entertained this thought in some form at some time? Yet to hear it directed aloud toward a human being was so offensive that for all its apparent piety it had the shock effect of profanity.*

We were flattered beyond measure when Mrs. Lee invited the two of us for dinner one evening. We drove behind her, following her small British car as she led us through down-town Kowloon. The night streets were a neon display of English and Chinese, and crowds of people moved past the shopfronts. Although it was almost nine o'clock, small children sat along the sidewalk eating rice or doing their homework, unconcerned by the darkness or the hour. I thought with a pang of our three, tucked in bed with strict instructions to stay there, with a baby-sitter watching. Was it possible to give children so much freedom? I felt torn between the impulse to pity them and envy them.

We arrived at an elegant Chinese restaurant. As we entered, Mrs. Lee apologized for not entertaining us in her own house.

"You'll find we very seldom invite foreigners into our homes," she said. "In most cases the contrast is too great. Even Chinese who have money do not decorate their houses on the scale that Americans do."

Gordon and I exchanged glances. Was tonight to be a social visit, or an extension of our training?

Mrs. Lee deftly ordered dishes in Mandarin while we sat overwhelmed by her linguistic ability. In addition to perfect English, she spoke French, German, and a variety of Chinese dialects.

The tea was poured and we formally drank to one another, holding the cup in both hands. There was polite chatter, asking how we liked Hong Kong and what we intended to do.

"I've been watching you two," she said slowly, "and I'm interested in what kind of approach you're going to take. You'll be working with Chinese young people in a high school?"

"Right, as a chaplain," said Gordon.

"I see . . ." She sipped her tea thoughtfully, the grim authority of her teacher face replaced by a look of perplexity. "How are you going to do this?"

"I beg your pardon?"

"How . . . I mean what are you going to give them?"

"As far as I know now, chapel every morning, Biblical knowledge classes, and hopefully do some counseling."

"Since you are a Westerner, do you think Chinese youngsters will confide in you?"

"I think they will—when I can speak their language."

"This is a church-related school?"

"Right."

"Then you should have a core of about ten per cent who will have some background. What I wonder is this . . . How do you convince the rest of the students that what you have to say is valid for them? There are several approaches that have been taken. One is to make them guilty by talking about sin and then offer Christianity as a cure for guilt. You see, we Chinese have no concept of sin as a state of being. We have our codes, and we live by them. Only those guilty of definite offenses, such as criminals, are considered sinners. If you tell a young person he is a sinner, he would be terribly offended. Of course, those brought up in the church will understand because they're accustomed to Western thinking and Christian terms. But then, they don't need you, do they? No . . . It's the other ninety per cent you will be interested in. You could tell them about the life and teachings of Christ, but how could you convince them that these are superior to the life and teachings of Confucius?"

She politely refilled our teacups, and continued,

"You could give them your ideas of heaven and hell, of punishment and reward in the hereafter, but we Chinese are not too concerned about those places. For the most part, we are a very practical people. What you say will have to be valid for the here and now as well."

"But the Christian life is more than—"

"The Christian life!" Mrs. Lee interrupted Gordon. "Are you going to teach them how to live a good moral life? We Chinese have a morality that I would say is at least as good as that of your culture. Our family ties are close. Our children are obedient. We have very little juvenile delinquency, and divorce is rare. Our old people are respected. What do you have to compare with this? Tell me, what do you honestly have to give these young people that is better than what they have?"

I opened my mouth and held up a finger, but she was not finished.

"There is one last approach that I advise you will not be effective . . . the idea that you are doing this for God. How can you expect people to respond to what you are doing for God? They become little more than objects by which you obtain God's favor . . ."

A dish of food arrived, greens with steamed shrimp. For a moment I was overcome with empathy for the small sea creatures, taken from their ocean, stripped of their shells, and left to lie hunched and naked in a strange world.

It was drizzling during the drive back to our apartment in Shallow Water Bay. I sat limply next to Gordon as he drove grimly, watching the road. There was a muffled quietness, with only the sound of the windshield wipers beating out a steady rhythm. I closed my eyes, trying to think coherently. The dream and the reality were out of focus tonight . . . There was the stark reality of which Mrs. Lee had reminded us. We were people from the Western world, illiterate, inarticulate, at the bottom rung of a new culture, unaware, insensitive, bigoted . . . Yet superimposed across this darkness was an aspiration, a dream of doing what would be difficult to do even in our own country where the language and customs were familiar: to search out what the love of God as expressed in Jesus Christ had to do with relationships between people, even people of different races and backgrounds.

There was one deeply puzzling factor. Our deepest motivation came from our Christian commitment, and yet it was our identification as Christian missionaries that made honest human relationships difficult. *How could we live out a positive affirmation of our faith without having it become a condemning force that provoked hostility and alienation? Was it the nature of faith to create barriers, or was true faith intended to eradicate barriers? And if so, how?*

I looked up at Gordon, driving grimly in the darkness, and knew that if there was a way he would find it . . . and I would find it with him.

2   BEYOND WORDS

The discoveries about words came in small lightning flashes, both about Cantonese words and the usage of words in any language.

In the beginning, words were all-important. They ruled our lives from morning until night. By eight-fifteen we were out of the door on our way to school, and at four o'clock in the afternoon we laid our books aside, too weary to concentrate any longer and ready for a change of pace.

One such day Gordon drove to Check Wan market to buy supplies. It was relaxing to stroll leisurely through the rows of stalls, to look at the endless variety of green vegetables and dried fish, to watch the village life come and go. He walked slowly, enjoying the sun and the sound of the sea just beyond the market.

At the end of the row of stalls stood the fresh fish market. A young boy sat out front on a rough wooden stool, reading a book. He, like every other boy on the street, had black hair and dark eyes, simple clothing and carefree rubber sandals. There was nothing that marked him out from the crowd, except his absorption in the book.

Gordon strolled by and glanced at the cover. The boy looked up sharply.

"Buy some fish, sir?" he asked.

"*M' sai, M' goi.*" Gordon thanked him in the negative, then continued in Cantonese, "I notice you're studying English."

"I go to night school," the boy replied. "I have to work during the day."

His English was very good. For a moment Gordon hesitated. Should he drop the Cantonese and converse in the more familiar language? No, he decided, he needed the practice.

"Why are you learning to speak Cantonese?" the boy asked. "We're all learning to speak your language so we can get better jobs and earn more money. But why should you trouble yourself to learn our words?"

"Because I'd like to be your friend," Gordon answered, "and I think I can get to know you better if I learn your language."

"That's true . . ." he said thoughtfully. "But why should you want to be my friend?"

"Why shouldn't I want to be your friend?"

The boy laughed, his dark eyes puzzled.

"Why do you come to Hong Kong? What work do you do here?"

"I work with a group of Chinese Christians."

"Oh, now I understand. You're a *Mok-si*, a pastor-teacher . . .

I knew a man like you once. Where do you speak your doctrine?"

"I don't speak anywhere yet . . . I'm only a student now. But when I finish I'll be teaching boys of your age. Are you sixteen?"

"Fifteen. Ah, then I may call you teacher. To be a teacher is a good thing. We Chinese respect our teachers highly because we believe that they show a concern for the next generation."

"And what may I call you?"

His eyes were wary for a moment, then relaxed in a smile.

"My name is Wong Wing Sung," he said. "Sometimes they call me Ah Sung."

"My Chinese name is Ding," Gordon said.

"Ah, Ding SinSaang! Will you come often and teach me English?"

"Your English is already excellent. Will you teach me Chinese?"

"It is good. You speak Chinese to me, and I will speak English to you. Then we can help each other."

They shook hands by the fish market and agreed, and a lasting friendship was begun.

We had known Wing Sung for several months when Gordon was invited to speak in one of the Chinese churches in Kowloon, across the harbor. Since Wing Sung had asked us where we "spoke the doctrine," we invited him to accompany us. Wing Sung was not sure. To study English on the street with a foreigner was strange enough, but to go to church was another matter.

After a few days' deliberation, he had his answer.

"I'll come if it rains," he promised Gordon, and that was how it was left.

When Gordon came home that day, he told me of Wing Sung's reply.

"Why would he say he'd come if it rained?" he mused. "I didn't want to ask him. He seemed to think I should know why."

"Oh, it's probably some superstition he has," I said easily. "You know, like leaving it up to fate, or something. Who can stop the rain?"

"I know. But you'd think that he'd say he would come if it didn't rain."

"Gordon, haven't you discovered yet that if you say it one way, the Chinese say it the opposite way? There's more to learning this language than the words you speak. You've got to have your brain put in backward."

"Maybe so," he said quietly, but I could see that he was not convinced.

On Sunday the rain was pouring down in tropical torrents. It had rained all night, and the streets were lined with flowing streams. People hurried into the church, armed with bright-colored umbrellas.

True to his word, Wing Sung met us at the door. It seemed strange to find him here in a setting so different from the market. The church was roomy and well-built, with a traditional Western sanctuary air about it. Wing Sung sat down a bit nervously next to me, and Gordon left us to don his robe and take his place on the platform.

The order of worship began, and I strained to catch a familiar sound. For the most part the words used in church were still unintelligible to me. Outside, at home and on the street, we had begun to converse, but the highly literary vocabulary used in church was almost another language. I sat miserably plucking at a tone here and a sound there, wondering if what I thought I heard was actually what was being said.

I glanced around. The people in church were generally well-dressed, perhaps businessmen or fairly well-to-do middle class, with a sprinkling of poorer people; but then it was hard to tell. An old woman in a black *sam-fu*, the commonly worn loose trousers and blouse, might be very wealthy, while a smartly dressed young woman might be a struggling student or a working girl.

The singing began, and Wing Sung found the page for me. He had never been in church before, to my knowledge, but he was far ahead of me in being aware of what was happening. He could read the words . . . to me they were baffling designs. He could tell if his hymnbook was rightside up or upside down, which, I discovered, was more than some people were able to determine. He became more relaxed, and I became more tense. The air between us changed. I was a Christian and he was not, but he was Chinese and I was not. He was in command.

A Chinese woman stood up to read the week's announcements, her clear flutelike tones coming over the public address system with fluid ease. I stared at the bulletin before me, realizing that each of those melodious tones was deciphered from one of the puzzling designs . . . My stomach twisted, and I felt agonizingly lonely and ignorant.

Little children walked about the church freely, and two old women behind us carried on a voluble conversation. Wing Sung leaned over and whispered loudly,

"Perhaps Ding SinSaang thought it strange when I said I would come here today if it rained. Please tell him the reason for this is that we don't catch as many fish when the weather is rainy, and my father can let me go for a few hours. If the shop is busy, then we all have to work."

I sat nodding politely, feeling privately chagrined by my previous easy explanation. What I had written off as possible superstition was actually a case of practical necessity. A family's livelihood was involved.

I looked around again, wondering how many of these people were from Wing Sung's social strata. Weekly morning services were a fixed part of traditional Christianity. If this continued to be so, how could Wing Sung and the thousands like him ever fit into the pattern? How could he ever become a Christian? Would God make it rain every Sunday morning at eleven o'clock?

Gordon was behind the pulpit now, and I checked my irreverent thoughts to smile encouragingly at him. He spoke in English, and the Chinese pastor translated into the dialect spoken by the congregation. Sentence by sentence the speakers gave the message. It was a long laborious process, with every switch of language causing a break in communication. I could see the perspiration standing out on Gordon's face, and knew he was dissatisfied with this method of speaking.

Someday he would have a full command of Cantonese ... He would speak fluently from the pulpit with no barriers of language. It would be a great day, a day worth working for ... But what about the wrong guesses, the inability to understand why a boy could come only if it rained? Would we ever be able to know the unspoken factors?

Other incidents both inspired and humbled us in our search for words ...

It was late fall, nearing the Western holiday of Christmas. The sun in Hong Kong had lost its stinging heat, and the afternoons were cool and crisp. One day I walked to the beach with our children and let them run to play in the sand while I wrote letters. I sat on the warm shore and watched the sea lap up in constant motion, allowing it to massage the tired tightness of my mind. It was good to write letters occasionally, if for no other reason than to force oneself to focus on what was being accomplished. In order to set thoughts down on paper they had to achieve some sort of organization, and often I felt more organized after writing to someone than before I started the letter.

I paused and looked out over the sand, checking on the children's whereabouts. Mike's towhead was practically buried in a sand tunnel he was digging, and the two girls were busy carrying water from the sea ... *How would it be for them to grow up here? How would it be for all of us to grow up here? They were as old in this culture as we were ... Perhaps they would understand it better than we ever would.*

Suddenly, my thoughts were interrupted by the sound of stealthy movement behind me. I looked up to find two small Chinese boys peeking over my shoulder at the paper on my lap.

"How are you?" I asked in Cantonese, quite proud of the fact.

They froze and stared at me, then disappeared around a beach house. In a few moments they were back with three other boys, and pointed at me.

"That Westerner speaks Chinese," they said in the beautiful clear tones.

"Of course I do, don't you?" I asked.

They doubled with laughter and began to tumble in the sand, showing off. I flipped the stationery over and began to sketch on the back of it the action and merriment of small boys on the sand.

"Not too bad," said a husky voice over my shoulder.

"Do you like to draw?" I asked.

"No, I like to light firecrackers," he said, and was gone. The next thing I knew there was a ring of little boys around me.

"Are you American?" they asked.

"Yes, I'm a *Meigwok Yan*."

"Are those your children? What do American children like to play? Do they play guns?"

"They like to play in the sand the way you do. Soon they're going to be getting ready for Christmas. Do you celebrate Christmas at your house?"

"No, we have Chinese New Year for our big festival. We hear that American children have many gifts at Christmastime. Why do they get gifts?"

I thought for a moment, sorting out the various reasons I had heard to find a feasible one.

"They get gifts because it's a birthday. Do you know who was born at Christmastime, whose birthday it is?"

"He does," said a boy, pointing to one of the group. "He goes to a Jesus-teaching school."

"Do you know the story about Christmas?" I inquired, stretching my vocabulary to its limit.

They took it as an offer.

"No. Tell us . . . Tell us a story . . ." came a chorus of young voices. "Tell us a story to let us listen!"

It was the sort of situation we had dreamed of, someone who really wanted to hear. Yet I felt as though I were on stage and had forgotten my lines. Why had I let myself get into this predicament? The word for manger—what was it? For angel . . . for shepherd . . . for any of the special Christmas terms? They were the next lesson in the book, and certainly not the kind of words one would pick up on the street. How could I tell them I did not know the basic story of the Christian faith?

They sat quietly waiting, running the sand through their fingers.

"Once, long ago . . ." I began, using the words from an oatmeal advertisement on Cantonese television, "there lived . . ."

Before many sentences, I incurred a linguistic snag. On sudden inspiration, or desperation, I turned to the boy who had been to the "Jesus-teaching school."

"—and do you know what happened next?" I asked enthusiastically.

His eyes brightened and he nodded vigorously, continuing the story where I had left off. I let him go as long as he would, then injected, "Right! And then what?" and he was off on a fresh start. Whenever he began to hesitate, I encouraged him to tell us what had happened next until he had completed the entire story. It was beautifully told in words that were on the little boys' level, and told by one of them. It was like speaking through another person's mouth words that I did not even know. It was like a miracle.

I gathered up the children and went home to fix the evening meal. I moved in a kind of daze, saying the new words over and over to myself until I knew them by heart. *Someday, I would be able to tell a story like that . . . as well as a fourth-grade child . . . but then I would have other experience and wisdom to add value to my words, would I not?*

Chinese New Year came on the heels of Christmas, with its icy winds and bright colors, and then the spring rains . . .

All day long the sky had been a gray slate, and the rain had made a sodden wash of the streets. By nightfall the radio was announcing the plight of the hillside dwellers. Several hundred people were homeless, and the areas were badly flooded.

We and our children were safe in the house, watching the rain beat down and wondering how much moisture the walls could take. Already the rain was seeping in around the windowsills and under the doors. The children were wide-eyed. We tried to put them to bed early that evening so we could study.

They knelt around me, saying their prayers. Marita and Michael were five, and little Deidra was barely four. The wind howled, driving the rain against the windows, and they scooted closer together for protection.

"I want you to remember something when you pray tonight, children," I said. "When you're in your warm beds, think of a lot of boys and girls who don't have their own beds to sleep in tonight. The rain washed their houses down the hillside. Don't you think you should ask God to take care of them tonight and help them find a place to sleep?"

Marita was on her feet in a second.

"I know, Mommy. I've got a better idea. Why don't we push all the furniture to one side and get some blankets and let a lot of people sleep here tonight? And then you could fix breakfast for them in the morning. Wouldn't that be a good idea, Mommy?"

"I . . . I don't think so, honey."

"But why not?"

"Well . . . People just don't do things that way . . . I mean . . . there are other neighbors in this building, and they might not like it if we took in a lot of wet, strange people . . ."

"You mean we *can't*?"

"I don't think so, hon. Come on now, let's say our prayers."

She stood with her hands behind her, refusing to kneel.

"But what if everybody said that?" she persisted. "Then what good would it do to pray?"

"We could pray for the rain to stop," I suggested.

"You can pray if you want, Mommy," she said with disgust, "but I wish I could do something!"

Gordon and I sat in the living room studying that evening, but my mind was not on the words.

Words . . . words . . . speak the words and stop the rain . . . Could it be that our concept of miracle, or what we expected God to do when we prayed, and our definition of mission were somehow correlated? Were we in an otherworldly state where we prayed and the rain stopped, where we spoke and the work was done? Was it all words?

The rain was still pouring down. I heard it and shuddered. It had not stopped.

I looked across the room at Gordon. He sat with his feet propped up, translating a page into Chinese.

"I wish we could do something," I said abruptly.

"Do what?"

"Oh— Work in a community center or church. Just some-place where we could feel more involved."

He looked across at me patiently.

"If we shoot off on all sorts of tangents we'll never be worth anything to anybody. As far as involvement, we'll have to wait and take things as they come. We can't go around forcing ourselves on people. Why don't we stick to it and do one thing really well first, like finishing this lesson tonight?"

I picked up my book, admiring and resenting his self-control. The words would be necessary; no one would deny that. Without them we would be deaf and mute, totally helpless in this new world. But what was this restlessness tonight, this uncertainty, this impulse to throw the lesson book out in the storm and see what it could do about the situation?

The rain battered at the bedroom windows, and I went to cover the children. Marita was asleep now like the rest, her impudent nose smashed against the pillow. I scanned her small face, a combination of tenderness and anger welling up inside me . . .

How would it feel to be huddled in the rain with three fright-ened children . . . cold . . . hungry . . . shivering?

I covered the last child, and stood in the dark and cried. For some things there were no words.

3   ARMS OF THE CROSS

Involvement came to us before we had expected, and from the most unlikely of our acquaintances. It began one morning around the thermos jugs and instant coffee at Old China Language School.

Mrs. Lee was sipping coffee with us, and we were all a bit on edge. It was odd how such a minute woman could terrify people twice her size. Perhaps it was a certain quality she carried about her, a quality of clean-burned truth, ruthless and relentless. Whenever I opened my mouth to speak to her, I had the feeling that my words were being judged and sorted and weighed, and often they came tumbling back on my head as shallow or thoughtless merely by the look in her eyes. But by the same standard that sham was rejected, an honestly spoken statement was accepted and became a victory of communication, rejoiced over and celebrated silently. She was more than a language teacher . . . she was a new awareness, a kind of second conscience to go with the new words.

We were complaining, that morning, about the lack of opportunity to use our Cantonese in the local churches.

"Every time I open my mouth and say *jo-sun*," Porter complained, "someone turns around and says, 'Good morning, sorry, I don't speak English.' It's the most frustrating thing. In the first place, I was speaking Chinese, and in the second place, how can somebody tell me in such perfect English that he doesn't speak English?"

"You fit into a pattern," said Mrs. Lee. "You're judged by your face and not heard."

I looked at Porter's face . . . an austere, frightened kind of face. Was he really trying to relate to the extent of saying good morning in Chinese? But what was it Wing Sung had said . . . *All foreigners know how to say good morning and garbage, but if you say anything else to them they only stare at you blankly* . . .

"But how can one break out of this?" Gordon was asking.

She turned and looked at him quizzically. "Why don't you come to my church?" she asked.

"Your church!" I gasped, and saw the ice in her eyes. She had read my mind. How could anyone as outspoken and critical and sophisticated as she belong to a church? The meaning of my question fell back on me, and I stammered, "I . . . I didn't know . . ."

"You didn't know I was a Christian?" She laughed. "No, maybe I don't fit your pattern either. To be part of something does not mean that one must be blinded to its difficulties or gloss over its problems. You might be surprised to know that I'm a deaconess."

I stood, blushing. Of course, how could she have known so much about various approaches unless she had observed both the Church and the Chinese community at close range? The average person on the street probably couldn't care less.

It was a few weeks later that Mrs. Lee repeated the invitation in a more serious tone.

"We're without a pastor," she said to Gordon. "Could you help us in this interim until we get another man?"

"I, help you?" Gordon said incredulously. "How could I? I'm only one year old in this culture, and there are people of middle age and older in your church. How could I be a pastor to them?"

Mrs. Lee's eyes were almost kind, and there was no rejection in them. "If you approach the task in that spirit you will find many willing teachers," she said, "and you will have much to give as well."

And so it was that Gordon became involved in the life of the Brotherly Love Church, one of the group of Chinese churches that had their origin in the missionary movement in China during the eighteen-hundreds. At this point it had become thoroughly indigenized, and was seeking, under the leadership of third- and fourth-generation Christians, to find its place in Hong Kong's society.

The Brotherly Love Church was located across the harbor in the heart of a Kowloon resettlement area. Row after row of government housing rose up from the street, festooned with washing and clattering with the sounds of human life. Children scampered over the sidewalks, and on the ground floor, shops laid out their wares for the residents to buy. Only one section of a city of four million, this was a town of 150,000, a teeming, ever-moving, noisy segment of humanity, pushed together, piled up, and crying out for life . . .

In the center of this area stood the church. A recent structure, it possessed a quiet white serenity in the midst of the frenetic life about it. Although the congregation as a fellowship had been in existence for over seventy years, this building had been theirs for only a few months, and the structure was a source of grateful pride to the members. But in choosing to build in this area, the group was also faced with a grave question. What connection was there between this serene white building on the corner and the complicated mass of humanity that began fifteen feet from the church door? Obviously, if the church were to belong to the community, there would have to be interaction . . . but how? Should the church seek primarily to draw the neighborhood into its meetings, or should the church itself go out and seek to relate to the complexity of the life of the community?

It was interesting to observe how the cross-currents of Christian thinking operated in this church. There were the faithful followers of missionary thinking, to whom the community was considered evil, a citadel of pagan darkness that must be cut off from the church lest its dedication be influenced. Only those who had fulfilled certain requirements would be allowed to enter the church or to become a part of the program.

Under such thinking ran another current. This was not so much a residue of missionary thought as it was the approach of the less religion-oriented businessmen in the congregation, and the youth. Their attitude centered more around a composite of being Chinese and the idea of God's love. These people saw themselves not primarily as Christian but as Chinese. Chinese were all of one blood, and if Jesus Christ loved one of them, he must love them all. If the Western concept of God as revealed in Jesus Christ was for one group of Chinese believers, then surely this good news was for the whole community of 150,000, and beyond that to the whole city and the world. These Christians had no concept of division, of exclusion, or of rejection.

Early in his experiences at the Brotherly Love Church, Gordon discovered this strain of thinking. In the youth group was a teenage boy from a Chinese Christian family. He had been taught in the Christian faith ever since infancy, baptized in the church, and attended Sunday School regularly. Yet for all his fervent faith in Jesus Christ, he had no concept of leaving the rest of the community out of God's love and concern. This was apparent one day when the decoration of a small chapel was under consideration. It was the responsibility of the youth group to design the room, and they had asked Gordon to help them. Remembering churches he had seen in his home town, Gordon suggested that they use a stylized cross, with an elongated upright and a short crossbeam, covering only the center portion of the front panel.

During the discussion the boy raised his hand.

"Ding Mok-si," he said shyly, "may I make a suggestion?"

"Please," Gordon said, happy for participation.

"If I were planning the cross, I would use a piece of wood that would reach all the way across the panel."

"But don't you think that might look a bit crowded?"

"I wasn't thinking about the style, but the meaning. If we have a three-foot panel and a one-foot cross, it will say to me every time I come here to worship that God's love is not big enough for everyone. I think the cross should be as wide as the area to be covered, even if it doesn't look as good."

We talked about the young man's comment. Was he closer to the truth than we dared to admit? Was there something about this Chinese cohesiveness of the human family that made him impervious to the division we felt so sharply between the churched and the unchurched?

I thought long and deeply about this perplexity. As a child and young person I had always been convinced that the world belonged to the devil, and that only as we won it for God did it become His. The world was evil, and we must stay clear of it as much as possible. Yet now, as an adult, there was always a kind of estrangement connected with my faith that troubled me, a hostility toward the world around me. If God was love, as

I also had been taught, how could I show this love while I had a submerged feeling of suspicion and hostility toward those who were not like me, who did not believe as I did? It always managed to show through at the wrong time, and I found myself condemning those my faith was teaching me to love. It seemed to be a built-in contradiction. The feeling of brokenness from other people filled me with fear . . . cut me off . . . put me on the defensive. And now, as a missionary, the situation was compounded. I had to believe that others were wrong in order to believe that we were right . . . in order to give validity to our existence. Hostility was a necessary part of my mission theology; and yet, to my horror, I found that when these thoughts were in my mind, I looked into Chinese faces with fear. We were of different origins, of different camps, and the confrontation was too awesome to bear.

One day as Gordon and I drove into the resettlement area, I was struck by the sheer numbers of people around us, people with beautiful faces, courageous spirits, living against tremendous odds, cramped into small quarters . . . yet remarkably pleasant, clean, courteous, gentle. Surely the spirit of God was here in some form, in some way that we in our rigidity could not define Him. For a moment I was filled with a strange wistfulness, an odd feeling that if God loved them it wasn't fair . . . that I was the one being left out of some hidden scheme. It was a feeling I had often had when listening to the parable of the Prodigal Son. There was something not quite right about that parable, something that did not square with other facets of my Christian thinking. The whole story was not quite fair. The younger brother had gone out and done as he pleased and was welcomed back as the hero, while the good self-sacrificing steady son was taken for granted. He had kept all the rules and had a miserable time, and what did he get for it? An invitation to dance at his brother's party. Secretly, I was angry at the father for being such a stupid old man, and I always wanted to side with the elder brother; and yet, deep down, I knew that until I could be happy about the ending of the parable I was missing the whole point of what it had to say about God's love.

I began to wonder now . . . Could the roots of that resentment lie in my Christian thinking, in the idea that some people are God's children and some are not? I had forgotten that while the younger brother was in the far country he was still a brother, still the father's son. He did not suddenly become a son when he returned and was reconciled. Could it be that God had reconciled children and unreconciled children, but that they were all of one family?

I shared this perplexity with Gordon, expecting disagreement.

"It's perfectly possible," he said calmly. "In fact, I've always believed that all men are God's children."

I accepted his answer with a sigh of relief, and tried it out the next time I walked down the street. It was amazing, even pretending that this barrier was gone, how the unidentified hostility melted. I was God's child, and the woman coming toward me with a baby on her back was God's child. There was a flow of love, and a bond I had never felt before. The strained reaching out toward a foreign face and a foreign religion was gone. In our roots, in our origin, we were one.

Now, I was able to see the elder brother for what he was . . . a steady citizen who was more careful for his exclusive position in the father's household than he was of love for his brother . . . and I no longer wanted to champion his cause. The father was wiser than I had ever dreamed, and I could accept the ending of the story as something truer than I had ever realized before.

I was barely over this hurdle when I was plunged into a new kind of loneliness, a terrifying sense of loss. If one did not go about trying to make God's children out of people, what was mission all about? What urgency was there, sufficient to make one leave home and country, to delve into a puzzling culture and learn a torturous language? What were our aims?

Again I asked Gordon, to whom these things seemed to come less painfully. Why were we in Hong Kong?

"To share the love of God," he said without hesitation.

"Of course," I said, and adopted this as a new slogan. We were in Hong Kong to share the love of God, but just exactly what that meant, I hadn't the foggiest notion. It was many months, even years, before I could give a concrete definition of those words, before they could take on strong unquestioned meaning in the center of my being.

The deeper we became involved in the local church structure, the more we appreciated the Chinese Christian's approach to faith and life. There was a tremendous sense of community, of the brotherhood of being Chinese. When a church tried to make anything but a Chinese out of a Christian, it seemed doomed to failure. One expression that amused us, and that seemed to be applicable in this context, was the saying, "*If a fish is in a pond and the pond dries up, what will you do? Spit on him to revive him? Throw him back into the river!*"

And this is what we saw the Chinese Church trying to do. It struggled to get out of the ponds that faithful representatives of another era had built for it, cutting it off from the flowing stream of Chinese life, and to get back into the river, knowing that it would only die when the ponds dried up or the foreigners stopped spitting on the fish. We saw the church reaching out into the community, its native cohesiveness enriched by Christian compassion, going into the resettlement houses, allowing students from cramped apartments to study in the church, dividing the chuch basement into classrooms for a day-care nursery. There were fingermarks on the new white walls of the church, but they stood as a seal that the church had become an integrated part of the throbbing life of the community . . . not a Sunday morning luxury, but an everyday necessity to many. All this was done to the personal enrichment of the core, the believing members.

Because of three small children at home I was not able often to accompany Gordon to the church. Several times a week he would mount his newly acquired motor scooter, buckle on his crash helmet, and roar off to cross the harbor ferry and find his way among the crowded streets to the church. Usually the Bible woman from the church accompanied him to help him find the more obscure addresses, and up and down the densely populated area they walked, calling on this member and inquiring about that relative until the day's work was done. During these days Gordon learned to pray in Chinese, to offer words of consolation, to listen to people's problems. Some persons in the neighborhood were old, and loved to have a young man visit; others were young, and worried about the future, about examinations, about jobs. The area was a compact sample of human life, congested into a few city blocks, a compressed sample of the whole range of human tears and laughter, joy and misery, birth and death. One could not walk here day after day without being overcome both by the magnitude and the futility of life.

One day an old grandmother invited the two of us with our children to come for tea. We parked our car near the church and walked down the street, winding our way through the children playing on the sidewalk. They were friendly children, and they gathered around us laughing and chattering. I looked at their lovely faces and the faces of our American children, and Carl Sandburg's affirmation passed through my mind.

> *There is only one child in the world,*
> *And that child's name is all children.*

The words filled me with an undefined longing for a world that was not . . . *How easy this is for us to believe! We see a child wounded in war and we weep. That child is our child, and that wound is in our heart, and we are pierced with sadness . . . But to say that there is only one man in the world, and that man's name is all men . . . this is too hard for us, too complex. Our cultures and races and religions have severed our hearts until we cannot enjoy the familial ties we recognize so instinctively in our children. As men we have many names. We see a man by another name killed in war, and we do not weep . . . we count his dead body as a victory and a token of our strength. Where does this begin, and where do we draw the lines?*

I glanced up at the church steeple with the cross on top. *Surely not here . . . not here where the symbol of God's supreme love is marked out against the sky . . . surely not here.*

4   TEN THOUSAND FACES

Ironically, it was not in the avoidance of words but in their pursuit that we began to realize involvement on a social level.

One Sunday our family walked single file through a rice paddy. On either side of us the small green shoots jabbed their points through the mirror surface of the water. I glanced around to be sure none of the children were lagging behind on the narrow slippery path.

"What do you call rice, Siu-je?" Gordon asked.

The teenage girl ahead of us turned around and smiled. She was our new Sunday afternoon tutor and guide, Jung Siu-je. For several weeks now we had met her in the New Territories where she lived high on a mountain. Every week she enriched our store of knowledge about Chinese life and sayings, the habits of the country folk, and the beliefs of her people. Today we were going up the long climb to the temple of ten thousand Buddhas, on the mountaintop across from her home.

Jung Siu-je tossed her black hair out of her eyes and picked up a tiny rice plant.

"Rice," she explained, "has many names that are not the same. If you talk about the plant, it is *woh*, if you speak of the raw rice grain, it is *mai*, but if you refer to cooked rice, then it becomes *faahn*."

I looked up at the top of the mountain we were approaching. *What induced people to climb mountains and learn languages? Was it the very undefined nature of the victory attained that tantalized one? Sometimes one climbed toward unknown territory for the sheer exhilaration of the climb . . . yet a part of the exhilaration was the expectation of discovery at the top of the mountain. What was at the end of this climb?*

We filed out of the rice paddy and up a steep incline. A small wooden store selling soft drinks crouched beside the path. Barefooted children stared at us, and a dog barked suspiciously. We walked on up the path, up and up the steps carved out of the mountainside. The steps were of packed earth, worn smooth by the feet of many people who came to the temple to say prayers or, as Siu-je explained, to have a picnic, depending on one's need.

We walked through a bamboo grove, the slender pale-green trees filtering the sunlight in lacy patterns. On the shaft of a tree near the path, characters were carved on the green bark.

"What does this say?" Gordon asked, stopping to examine the tree.

Jung Siu-je blushed. "It's the name of a boy and girl who are friends," she said.

A strange warm sensation crept to my head and lodged somewhere between my ears. Here in a bamboo grove, carved in delicate characters, or hacked out on an appletree in an American orchard, or scribbled on a backyard fence or a subway wall . . . Was there any difference? Human love was a universal language, surrounding the whole world.

The temple of the Buddhas was a sprawling affair, perched on a plateau at the top of the earthen stair trail. A pagoda stood at one end of the clearing, a tall temple at the other. Inside the temple a huge Buddha sat in golden repose, staring blandly out over the magnificent valley scene before him. On the wall behind and to the sides was a geometric design, which, when the sunlight cleared from our eyes, we could see was numerous shelves of tiny carved images of the Buddha.

"Every one is different," explained our guide," and has been made by hand."

I looked closely at the images. There were row upon row of figures representing thousands of hours spent in painstaking labor, each piece the product of some man's concept of the Buddha, the Enlightened One, the One who understood the nature of God and man. But there was a striking alikeness in the carved images. Each one had an attitude of repose, of seeming resignation. Did not this in itself date the images in an age when enlightenment was identified with action, with man's ability to control and influence his environment? How could enlightenment be shown by staring into space?

I asked Jung Siu-je these questions, and she smiled softly.

"You from the West do not understand these things," she replied.

A little old nun in a gray robe appeared out of the shadows and bowed smilingly to Gordon. He smiled back, and began speaking to her as though she were his grandmother. I watched him for a moment, marveling at his ability to relate so well to so many kinds of people, and with no apparent sense of judgment or censure. How could he be such a committed Christian and yet so relaxed in conversation with a Buddhist nun? I found my natural reactions frozen in this situation. A Buddhist nun or monk was a strange, frightening creature to me, weird, mysterious, representative of either occult powers or false pretenses. When I saw the shaved head and the robe I wanted to look the other way, to ignore this creature whose ideas were opposed to mine.

But here Gordon was, talking to her, admiring the smooth polished seeds of her prayer beads as he would have admired a piece of costume jewelry . . . and she was patting him on the arm like any old lady would. Suddenly, I saw her as a human being instead of as a member of a religious order, and there was no need to look the other way. I was not afraid.

The children ran down the steps to investigate a huge mythical doglike creature standing in the courtyard. They climbed up to sit on its back and poke their fingers into its fierce-looking teeth.

"Should they do that . . . ?" I asked uncertainly.

"Leave them alone, they don't understand," Siu-je said with a smile.

"Are you Buddhist?" I asked.

"Not particularly," she answered. "My family worship in this way, but I've heard many things now."

"Are you a Christian, then?"

"Not yet," she answered again, slowly. "I've heard the Christian way, but I've not yet received baptism."

"Are you thinking of doing so?"

She looked out over the valley and did not answer for a moment.

"It's very difficult for one to make a decision like this alone," she said. "My mother is a strong Buddhist, and my father has died recently. If we became Christians we could not honor his death in the Buddhist way, and my mother's heart would be very sad . . . and I . . . I am her daughter. How can we live in the same house and worship different ways? Could I honor God by showing disrespect for my mother?"

The reaction of a Chinese person when asked if he were a Christian was quite different than one would expect when asking this same question in the context of a country that, true or not, thought of itself as a Christian culture. In the United States I had been more hesitant to ask this question because it carried a stigma, an evaluation of the individual's personal goodness. But in a Chinese setting, the question was more for identification. If one were a Christian, he thought a certain way and did certain things. He was identified with a certain group, but the superiority of this group was not taken for granted. The question was only a classification, not a stigma-loaded inquiry, and therefore not an invasion of one's privacy. It was more like asking what brand of soap one used than asking if one washed his face.

That day was a special occasion for our family. We had been invited to the Jung home for a meal. With Mrs. Lee's words that this was not done echoing in our ears, we took the invitation as a definite privilege and were anxious that everything would go according to the best manners. We had anticipated that the children might have trouble with Chinese foods to which they were not accustomed, and had prepared them in advance with careful instructions to eat whatever was set before them.

"But what if I can't stand it?" little Deidra asked tearfully.

"We'll give you ten cents for each dish you try," we promised.

The home on the mountainside was a neat wooden structure of three rooms in a straight row, a porch, and a cockloft where the smaller children slept. Mrs. Jung, the mother, was a widow with five children. A few of them had now reached teen-age, and were able to supplement the family income with small jobs.

Mrs. Jung met us at the gate, her thin face wreathed in a welcoming smile. One of the boys appeared from around the house and shooed away the goose that was honking at us and flapping its wings like a feathered watchdog.

"We keep the goose to scare away snakes," Mrs. Jung explained. Her Cantonese was heavily accented with a country dialect, and Jung Siu-je had to translate her words into the language we were just struggling to learn. The whole process was like trying to find a needle in the dark by the light of a candle that had gone out.

Our children busied themselves in getting acquainted with the Jung children and petting the numerous cats on the porch, while we went into the house. In the center of the living room stood a large portrait of the deceased father, still commanding the respect of his family. I could almost feel his presence in the house. It seemed morbid at first, and then I thought of the sons growing up in this room. They would never feel fatherless. In a strange sort of way he was there, in the center of all they did . . .

After long conversation and many cups of tea, dinner was served. The table was small and we crowded around it, bumping knees in order to reach the food. The children took advantage of this circumstance. Each time they tried fried beancurd or mushrooms or sweet lotus-seed soup, they would poke us under the table, which meant *chalk up ten cents for me, please*. But their enterprising spirits flagged when Mrs. Jung, seeing how well they ate, piled more into their rice bowls. They looked helplessly at us, and we looked at the Jung children. What were they doing? They seemed to come and go as they liked, and eat what they pleased, so we decided to let our youngsters do the same. There was no point in being more Chinese than the Chinese. After checking with us once more to see that they would still get paid, they slipped off to pet the cats.

A few weeks later Mrs. Jung repaid our visit. After the customary tea and politeness, accompanied by a gift of fruit and rice wine, she had a request to make. Since her husband's death, it had been hard for her to support the five children and care for them at the same time. There were factory jobs, but if she did this type of work, there was no one at home to look after the children. Did we know of any kind of work she could do? She was skilled in dressmaking and handiwork of various kinds, but had no outlet for her products. Could we help?

We immediately called up a friend who operated a Family Service Center and asked if she could help Mrs. Jung.

"I hardly know what to say . . ." Her voice hesitated. "There are five or six widows now who have come to me for this type of work, and our staff are all as busy as I dare to make them. If only we had someone to help out we could start a new group . . ."

I held the phone, waiting for the words, and they came.

"Could you help us?"

"I . . . I could try," I heard myself saying.

And that was how the dressmaking began.

The Family Center was a large organization, and the six women, including Mrs. Jung and me, were only a small corner. The first day I walked into the workroom, I did so with a great deal of trepidation. My Chinese was still halting and their English was nil. An added complication was the strong country dialect several of the women spoke, and others who spoke mostly Mandarin. Would we be able to communicate?

I spread out the design for a dress I had taken along, and they brought me a steaming amber glass of tea. I showed them paper dress patterns, which they had never seen, and demonstrated how they were used. In return they showed me samples of their handiwork to prove that they were skilled with their hands. They were more than anxious to help me speak, and when I would start a sentence and come to a dead impasse, they would fill in the missing words. Nouns such as straight pin and dart had not been in the language school vocabulary, and they laughingly supplied them when I paused and looked helpless. Imagine a grown woman who did not know what to call a straight pin! But by the end of the first get-together, an air of warm geniality had been created, and I left smiling inside out. We each had something to give and much to learn.

The project opened many ways of getting to know Hong

Kong. The retail buyers had to be approached to see if they liked the designs. We made a Chinese doll to go with each dress, and a man had to be found to make a rubber stamp of the doll's face so that they would at least look related to each other after being embroidered by six different women. We had to find materials, and this took us to the back streets and small alleys to hunt for good cloth at wholesale prices. Many of these merchants did not speak English, as did the merchants on the main streets, and I was forced to use Chinese. I was accustomed to hearing Gordon called *Ding SinSaang*, but I had had little occasion to use my Chinese name. Now the words *Ding Tai* became a familiar sound, and I began to respond to them almost as naturally as to my English name.

Tongue in check, we rushed where sensible people would have feared to tread. We bought cottons by the bolt and patterns by the handful. We set up a production line. Each woman would cut out six dresses and six dolls, take them home for a week, and then bring them back to the center for inspection and packing. We proudly chose a brand name, and ordered tags to sew inside the neck of our dresses.

Even Gordon became enthusiastic about the project. When our friend at the center saw this, she drafted him for another piece of work. A group of men out in the New Territories, refugees from China since the defeat of the Nationalist armies, were now old and in poor health. Would Gordon like to design some products for them to make?

It was the first time I had ever seen Gordon with his long legs poked under a sewing machine. He designed red potholders with Chinese characters for LOVE on them, hunted around the back alleys for leather to make coin purses, and came up with a host of other marketable and unmarketable ideas. The books were neglected outside of formal hours, but the words were being found in context . . . the context of real life and the social situation.

Was this not what words were for? How could one learn the words without learning the context in which they were spoken? And if one glimpsed the situation, it was impossible to refrain from involvement without somehow repressing and negating the whole natural flow of growth. To understand people's words meant to understand their problems.

The first week the women came back with dresses amazingly constructed. The sample I had shown them of my own work had been the design, but the inside was raw and unfinished. Theirs were as beautiful inside as outside. One of the women who had worked at the center for years was inspecting the others' work. She by chance picked up mine, turned it inside out, and said.

"Whose is this? It certainly wouldn't pass Ding Tai's eyes!"

The women in our group looked at me, and we shared a silent laugh over a ridiculous situation that required no words to express it. Perhaps they needed a designer, but the designer needed finishers!

It was this spirit of interdependence that bound us together in a common oneness. Even our fears were interrelated. They were apprehensive that their work would not pass inspection, and I was apprehensive that the design would not sell. Then one day I opened the Hong Kong newspaper to the fashion page and saw our dresses featured on a model, recommended by the fashion editor as a good buy. I brought the paper to the women, and we spread it out like an eager group of children reading comics.

"There we are!" I laughed. "You're famous!"

"*Chut meng* . . . famous . . . very famous!" they joked, and we walked about the workroom drinking tea and congratulating one another. We had done it! We were in business!

Every week the women returned with their dresses, and we began to know one another well. There was Mrs. Chun with her six children to clothe and feed and educate. There was Mrs. Wong who was often absent because her youngest had fevers. There was Mrs. Wai whose hands trembled and whose eyesight was poor. And there was wiry Mrs. Jung, the catalyst. Each week as I watched them work, I grew to admire them more. They were brave women, caught in the crush of a changing society, deprived of their husbands while raising families . . .

women who would have had every right to give up, but who did not. They worked far into the night over their treadle machines, stitching as though the fabric of their family existence depended on it . . . and by the look of the garments they produced, I could not doubt the quality of their family life.

Often while working with the women, I wanted to ask them about their beliefs, to verbalize the concern I felt for their spirits as well as for their physical well-being. Yet in some way it seemed redundant to speak, like the prosaic explanation of an exquisite poem The fact that I was Christian, that I was involved with them in a real life struggle, that I cared, that it mattered to me whether or not their six dresses passed inspection and they went home with a week's wages in their pocket . . . was this not enough?

Once when the occasion presented itself, I ventured to ask what one of the women believed.

"I believe in a good night's sleep. That would be my idea of heaven," she said, and the other women laughed sympathetically.

I could see her, sewing until two o'clock in the morning after putting a family to sleep, and I said no more . . . Perhaps God, for her, was not words . . . Perhaps He was rice and school uniforms and shelter for her young . . . Perhaps only as He came to her in these forms would she understand Him, or have any ability to hear Him . . .

And yet sometimes when the dresses were cut and the fabric closets were shut, when the women were going home and it was over for the day, I wondered . . . I wondered where they went and what their homes were like. I wondered how many little hands helped to embroider the faces on the dolls and how many fingers were pricked. I wondered many things, and felt a wistfulness, like a shadow, as I watched them go. That God loved them, I had no doubt. How could He help it? But that I was still separated from them by a wide gap, this I also knew.

What had happened? I had felt nearer to them when we passed on the street and smiled as strangers. Now that we were in closer confrontation, the gap yawned sickeningly. What was it that stood between us? It was as though we were relatives out of touch.

I went on with the motions, aware that within this framework there was the potential for satisfying relationships . . . Yet as a person I was not ready to understand it, not able to grasp its full significance.

5 RELATIONSHIPS

Suffering is a lost opportunity for most of us. We read of the courage of those who faced lions and fire for the cause of Christ, and with the rosy haze of time blinding our eyes we envy them, or sigh with relief that being a Christian today does not require any suffering. In fact, the very comfortableness of Christianity disturbs some of the more restless spirits, and we have a guilt about not suffering. Is there some way we can suffer and thus prove our loyalty, our genuine devotion, to what we believe?

In response to this inner restlessness, some of us invent ways to suffer. We make our lives miserable with introspection and hairsplitting, with rule-keeping and forms of punishment. Something within us tells us that if Christ suffered, to follow him we must also suffer, or we are superficial.

But why did Christ suffer? Was it not his closeness to God the Father and his complete identification with the plight of man that tore his heart? A loose connection on either end would have eased his suffering . . . but as he was truly united to God and man, the broken relationship between them, between God and man, between man and man, was his strongest grief.

As Christians, we began to see that suffering need not be sought for to be authentic. All one need do was to try relating honestly to those about him, with deep concern for the human predicament. It cost us all the suffering we could bear . . .

Gordon's involvement at the Brotherly Love Church led to another request: that he be chaplain and friend to a group of teenage boys in the old section of Kowloon City. These students were learning motor mechanics as a trade to prepare themselves for earning a living in the complexity of big city life. On a

narrow street in Kowloon City, a small building jammed between other buildings, covered with business signs and name
shingles . . . this was where the boys lived. Part of the building
was used for dormitory, part for classrooms. Under the windows
an assortment of vehicles was parked for repair, nearly blocking
the pedestrian flow on the already congested street.

Here, amid the constant city noises, the smell of pungent
cooking, the rustle of people moving, and the roar of motors,
Gordon met with the students several times a week. One session
was a Bible study, the next a discussion of their life as they
saw it.

The students were a muscular, sturdy, bright-eyed lot, who
ate three or four hearty bowls of rice at a meal, sang lustily,
and constantly played pranks on one another. Sometimes Gordon
arrived early and found them still in their greasy overalls, not
yet ready for the study session. He would join them in the
garage, laughing and joking.

It was difficult to know what relationship to have with these
students. That Gordon wanted a good relationship was a fore-
gone conclusion, but as time passed, what was to be defined as
"good" grew more complex. This became evident in the matter
of names.

Gordon began by saying,

"I'd like to know all of your names so we can get acquainted.
I'm Gordon—"

"Aren't you a *Mok-si?*" someone asked, using the name for
pastor.

"Yes, but you may call me by my first name."

"Oh . . . we can't call a *Mok-si* by his first name. It would be
disrespectful. Besides, you are older than we are. We should
either call you *Mok-si* or *SinSaang*. Our parents would be angry
if they knew we called you by your first name."

But Gordon, who was reaching for horizontal relationships
in which the lower and higher elevations would be flattened
out, insisted.

One day he noticed that the boys had nicknames for one
another.

"What is your nickname for me?" he asked.

The boys laughed and replied.

"Sometimes we call you old Ding . . . and sometimes we call you the shinyheaded monk."

Gordon came home crushed. He had meant to put himself on a level with the students, but they seemed to be poking fun at him. What had he done wrong?

We talked to Mrs. Lee. Her black eyes rolled, and she dilated her nostrils as she did when she smelled danger.

"Ah . . . Gordon!" she breathed. "Don't you see what you've done? You've stepped in and destroyed these boys' whole sense of right and wrong. They wanted to place you in the proper niche in their social pattern, and your niche was a high one. But when you refused, when you negated your proper place in their minds, they didn't know what to do with you. You were a misfit! All they could do was joke about something they had never encountered before. You've confused them!"

"But what should I do?" Gordon asked. "I don't want to place myself above them . . . How can I relate in that way?"

"No, but neither do you want to place yourself below them. You need not capitalize on their honor, that I appreciate. But neither should you allow them to despise you. In our thinking, familiarity should breed respect, not contempt."

"Where should I begin?"

"Perhaps you're too concerned about names. Just try relating and let them name you . . . And when they give you a name, don't correct them."

It was then that Gordon's motor scooter began breaking down. It broke down with regularity two or three times a week, and of course needed boys to fix it. There were boys coming on the back of the scooter, boys staying for dinner, and even an occasional boy overnight. Gordon not only prepared talks in Cantonese, he came home with grease on his clothes. He went home with some of the boys on days when they visited their families. He took a weekend trip with the boys to the Portuguese Province of Macao, and ate breakfasts of rice gruel and long fried doughnuts. The boys began to know him as a person, instead of as a misplaced social oddity. And strangely enough, most of them drifted back to calling him Ding *Mok-si*, or pastor Ding . . . and this time Gordon did not object. If it was a good name to them, let them use it. They were friends now, and names did not matter.

With the increased flow of traffic in our apartment, I began to think of redecorating it. With more ambition than money, I went looking for cotton yard goods to make new curtains and bedspreads, convinced that the apartment that housed us and our guests needed a more cheerful appearance.

One day I tramped the streets in the western end of Hong Kong Island for hours. Everything I saw was either ugly or too expensive. Up and down the streets I went, pinching fabric here, testing colors there, trying my Chinese on the shopkeepers in the little open-front stalls. Finally, at a tiny hole-in-the-wall shop I found cloth at a price I could afford, and bought an armload. Triumphant, I stopped at the thread stall next door, staggering under the weight of the package, and ordered six spools of thread.

"Oh, you better take one dozen," said the girl, eying the packages.

I counted my change. If I took more thread there would not be enough for bus fare home.

"No . . ." I hesitated. "I'd better keep enough for bus fare."

"Bus fare?" The girl looked at me incredulously. "You got a car parked up on the big street . . . you Americans got plenty money. Ha!"

I picked up the bundle and walked away, feeling angry. Suddenly, I turned around and looked at the stall where she worked . . . at the place where she undoubtedly lived. There was not even a window, much less a curtain. How could she understand a person who had just bought an armload of cloth and could only afford six spools of thread? Where were her curtains?

I stood on the street, two images swirling about in my head . . .

a frugal, thrifty housewife . . . and a rich snobbish foreigner. The disparity made me dizzy, like seeing a different image with each eye, and the proud acquisition of a few minutes before hung in my arms like a heavy burden.

How was relationship possible in a world so out of balance? To be so spartan on one scale, so superfluous on another . . . Surely relationship could not be measured in terms of goods, or what one had. If it must, there could be no rapport between people . . . Was there not some more basic measurement?

I got on the bus, feeling hot and weary and defeated, and sat down under the bundle of cloth. For a wild moment I wanted to open the window wide and throw it all away . . .

This emotion deepened several weeks later when we awoke one morning to find our home a shambles. The kitchen screen had been cut by a knife slash. Gordon's watch was taken from the bedside stand in the room where we had been asleep. Our closet was ransacked and the kitchen floor was a jumble of brief cases, purses, a typewriter, and our tape recorder. Evidently our night visitor had been frightened and dropped his loot to escape.

To have this happen just when we were so anxious to feel a part of the people around us was most disconcerting.

"Gordon, do you think it's because we fixed the house up?" I asked worriedly. "Do you think we look like we're loaded?"

"Don't worry about that," he said. "We've got to be ourselves too . . . But I don't think we should keep anything valuable in the house. What about the silver?"

"Get rid of it," I said. "Do we have anything else?"

That week we sorted through our possessions, disposing of or sending to our parents anything we were afraid of losing. When our house was stripped down to the functional living necessities and work materials, we breathed a sigh of relief. If we wanted to build fearless relationships, we could not filter our friends . . . and if we did not filter our friends, we could not have the kind of environment that would tempt those who had less than we did to help themselves. As for what was left, if anyone needed it worse than we did, he could have it . . . although preferably not in the middle of the night.

When possessions stood in the way of open relationships, one had to weigh priorities. Was not the ability to trust people in itself a priceless possession . . . ? Not a simple trust that everyone was good, but a kind of tough trust of people, as they were . . .

We discovered many angles about relationship in regard to possessions. The Chinese concept of borrowing and repayment among friends and family is very different from that of the West. If a man is in need, he "borrows" in order to save himself the pain of begging. But the basic idea is that a friend who can loan owes it to the friend who is destitute, and he must not expect repayment, for he himself may someday be in the place of the borrower. No debt or loan is an incident in itself, but a continuous relocation of needed possessions among friends.

At first we did not understand or even know this. When, therefore, we were approached by one of the young boys in Gordon's group for a loan to cover an emergency, we gave it to him on the boy's solemn promise to repay. Soon weeks had passed, then months, with no sign of repayment.

One day Gordon confronted the boy.

"I think you should try to start paying back what you've borrowed," he said. "It's not the money I'm concerned about, but your character."

The boy smiled, a look of relief on his broad tan face.

"Ah . . . Ding Mok-si! That makes me so happy! As an American, I thought it was the money you would be worried about. But don't worry about my character. My character is fine!"

And according to his rules, it was. Gordon had offered himself as a friend and had been taken at his word. At first this seemed unfair, but later when Gordon and I discussed this, there was a familiar ring to it. Who had said, "When you loan, do not expect repayment . . ."? Perhaps it was foreign to us only because we had not taken these words seriously. We had pushed them aside as one of the more impractical sayings of Jesus Christ . . .

Then there was the evening we invited the Indian army officers over for a roast beef dinner. It was the best meat we could find, and although we knew some Indians would not eat beef, we ignored the fact. Since these men were our everyday acquaintances in Language School, we thought they would be quite sophisticated about such things, army life being what it is. We were all basically quite alike, were we not?

But when we sat down to eat, one of the handsome young Indian men took one sniff of the beef and asked,

"Is this mutton?"

"No . . ." I said, warning bells ringing in my brain. "It's . . . beef."

A look of revulsion crossed his face, and he laid down his fork.

"Shall I scramble an egg for you?" I asked hurriedly.

He nodded weakly, still looking a bit sick.

I stood in the kitchen, jabbing fiercely at the eggs. Were people actually all alike, or was this a crazy mixed-up world where goodness and flavor to one person was repulsion to another? Was there no reliable common bond between us as persons? Then it came to me . . .

Everyone does have an alikeness, but this does not mean that they are all like me. We have an alikeness, but it is different from any of us individually . . . an alikeness outside of us all . . . a common point that we all face, but on which none of us stands squarely. We have been created in the image of God, and it is God-likeness we share, however tainted and tarnished. This can be our only alikeness. Thinking that people are all like me can lead only to disillusionment. Am I the center of the Universe . . . ?

Several weeks had passed since we saw Wing Sung when he telephoned us one day.

"Could you come to Check Wan beach for a barbecue?" he

asked. "I can get some chicken wings and sausages here in the market, and we can cook them over an open fire."

At first we wanted to refuse, knowing the meat would cost him more than a day's wages. Then we realized he wanted to repay in some way for the times he had eaten at our house, and we accepted.

The day was sunny and bright and the beach was lovely. Large waves pounded up on the shore, spraying whiteness against a perfect blue sky. The children were busy spearing chicken wings dipped in peanut oil and soy sauce and roasting them over the open fire. Wing Sung was everywhere, helping this one and advising that one. I watched him, strong and brown under the sun, and thought what a good friend he had become. Somehow he did not seem like a visitor . . . he was a part of the family.

Gordon came to where I stood and whispered quietly,

"Do you see that man over there? What's he doing?"

I looked. Crawling across the beach toward us was a thin, haggard figure. He stopped and held out his hands to us, called out, and then began dragging himself again. Gordon dropped his roasting stick and walked toward him.

"Be careful! . . ." I said quietly. One never knew when such a man was putting on a begging act, or perhaps had something contagious.

Gordon reached the man where he lay in the sand and examined his leg. It was bluish and swollen, with the toes protruding at an odd angle.

"I broke my leg . . ." the man said. "Three days ago I broke my leg and couldn't walk for help. No one would help me. They thought I was a beggar pretending . . . I've had only breadcrusts left by picnickers for three days. Please help me . . ."

We cooked some food for the man, which he devoured rapidly. The picnic had taken on a different feeling in the presence of the man's misery, and we too ate hurriedly and rubbed out the fire. Wing Sung and Gordon carried the wounded man to the car, and we drove him to the hospital.

When Gordon signed the paper for his admission, the attendant looked at him quizzically.

"What are you to this man?" he asked.

"A friend," Gordon answered.

The following morning Wing Sung came back to our house. My eyes were sore and my throat was raw and scratchy. He took one look and said, "*Ah yah!* It's the smoke from yesterday's barbecue. You've got hot air in your eyes. I know what to do for hot air."

"Oh, never mind," I said. "I'll just take a few aspirin and be all right."

"No! Aspirin are no good for hot air. Let me go to the herb shop and get some dried chrysanthemum flowers to make tea for you. That's what you need."

Against my protest he bought the flowers and carefully boiled up a tea. When he brought it to me, I was tempted to laugh. It looked like the water in which cut flowers might have stood for a week. Could I really drink it?

I took one glance at his kind concerned face, and drank it. In a few hours my eyes were clear and the sore throat was gone . . . and I was amazed!

That afternoon I thought about the man on the beach, and about the chrysanthemum tea. *Perhaps this was what relationship meant . . . trust. To be able to give help and take help . . . to be willing to sign one's name as friend of a stranger . . . to believe that flower tea was as good as aspirin. Perhaps this was how relationship worked at the zero point.*

Mrs. Lee's visit that evening was as welcome as it was unexpected. We were feeling high on the wine of having succeeded, of having related on levels we had never dreamed even existed. We poured tea and sat down to talk.

"It's strange how this works," I confided to her. "We find that relationships with our Chinese friends are always creative. They have a certain dimension to them that simply cannot come unless two cultures are crossed."

"Why do you think this is so?" she asked keenly.

"I've been analyzing this, and I would say its cause could lie in this direction. When two persons have matching cultural or religious assumptions, they often do not relate deeply. They tend to trade assumptions, to communicate on the surface in abbreviated symbols that have lost much of their original meaning. But when there are not assumptions in common, when the abbreviated symbols and sayings bring nothing but a blank stare, we must either communicate on a deeper and more original level, or grossly misunderstand each other. These deeper relationships with Chinese people can be wonderful or devastating, but certainly never dull . . ."

I paused, sensing a coolness in her eyes.

"You are doing well, so far," she said. "But why do you feel that this is particularly true about your Chinese friends?"

"I beg your pardon?"

"Why do you still categorize people? Unless you can take what you learn about relationships and apply it to your own countrymen, even to your own family, you are merely in another, more subtle state of prejudice. Until the day you can greet a man as a man and not be conscious of his face, except for its individual beauty, you are still acting as a judge . . ."

After Mrs. Lee left that evening I was, as usual, angry with her. What did she expect? Did she not appreciate the fact that we had already stretched our hearts and minds to the bursting point? After giving her several unvoiced pieces of my mind, I began to think about the truth of her words. What had we learned about relationships that could be applied in other areas, in any area with any kind of people . . . a key formula for relationship?

I took a pen and wrote hastily, the words coming from outside my conscious mind:

> *Perhaps it means stepping up,*
> *Or stepping down,*
> *The direction is not important.*

What is important is that I find myself in line,
Eye to eye with the person,
Not as a pose,
As condescension, or as pretense,
But that in a quiet moment of revelation
I know that I am him and he is me,
And there is no difference between us to God . . .
    Even if this clashes
    With what I thought I knew about God.

I laid the pen aside and looked at the words, wondering why I had written them. They felt true and frightening and almost unacceptable.

6   SHORT-CIRCUITED MIRACLES

The formal language study was coming to a close. Soon Gordon would preach his first sermon in Cantonese for one of the large congregations of the Chinese Christian Church. This climactic occasion would not only mark the end of formal study, but would also be viewed as a kind of initiation into the working life of the institution.

The sermon required careful preparation. Many evenings after market hours Wing Sung came to our house to help Gordon go over the characters. I watched the two of them at the dining-room table, poring over the sounds and tones, and wondered what was going on in Wing Sung's mind. Did he believe what he heard, or was this a purely linguistic effort? When he read clearly from the Chinese Bible, checking the characters with Gordon, I listened . . . Wing Sung was the teacher, Gordon the learner. Wing Sung was not consciously receiving, he was giving, and he was enjoying it. I marveled how one can win by losing, can give by taking. Gordon was actually allowing Wing Sung to teach him the Christian faith!

For my part, the long struggle for words had left me with a strange sense of loss. Gordon and I had studied together like brothers, competing and being tested with the same tests. Now he was receiving a test that I was not. He would be established in a given job, and I must find my own identity. By instinct I turned to my children, to my womanhood, to the interests that would make me a person in my own right. As a badge of my differentness from Gordon, I decided to grow long hair and bear another child, to be totally feminine after the long grueling hours in the tiny classrooms. Perhaps after reaffirming myself, I could go on and make some kind of contribution.

When I was assured that the new little "Ding" was on the way, we hired a girl to help with the household duties. One evening when Wing Sung was working with Gordon, he went into the kitchen to get a drink of water. I heard voices and listened to the exchange . . .

"Do you really believe what that *Mok-si* says?" the helper asked.

"I'm not for or against anything, but will follow the superior way," he replied, quoting an old saying.

I caught my breath. To witness to the love of God in Jesus Christ was so much more than saying it. Wing Sung was in our house often, and would judge the Christian faith by what he saw of us. It was almost too much responsibility to bear.

Everywhere we went, Gordon accumulated friends. One day we took the children past a small shop on a narrow street. There were shoes in the window, shoes that appealed to the little girls, so we walked in. When the transaction was completed, we had two pairs of shoes, and the shoe salesman had Gordon's promise to teach him English.

". . . but the only time I have left is before breakfast," Gordon warned him. "The rest of the day is full. Can you be ready at six o'clock to study until seven?"

"Oh, yes, yes!" he said enthusiastically. "That will be fine."

For several weeks Gordon was up early. Ah Chun, the short, round shoeman, met him in the park nearby and they talked in English for an hour. Every morning Gordon felt a bit more weary, but he would not give up. Finally, he came home one morning with a relieved grin.

"Ah Chun quit," he said. "His wife says he's getting too hard to live with."

The lessons were over, but the friendship continued.

Gordon's propensity for friends became a part of our routine. One day he called from the central part of town.

"I don't know what to do," he said. "I found this little fellow begging on the street, and he says he has no parents. I've contacted a social agency, but it's too late to take him anywhere tonight. Would it be all right if I brought him home for dinner?"

"Sure," I said.

But when he walked in, I actually did not know what I saw. Never in our years of Hong Kong life, or before that, had I ever seen such a woebegone, bedraggled, soiled-looking boy. He was large for a Chinese twelve-year-old, and had a deep base bullfrog voice. His face was burned to a dark brown from exposure to the sun, and he had the puffy look of too much rice and too little else.

At dinnertime he ate ravenously, and then promptly vomited. Gordon gave him a scrubbing, and took him out for a walk on the beach.

"Are you a plainclothes policeman?" the boy asked.

"No . . . why do you think so?"

"Because they said the police would be after me."

"Who said?"

"The men who made me carry the white powder."

"Opium? Why do you carry it for them?"

"They beat me if I don't . . . and they said if the police catch me they will kill me."

The boy's eyes were dark with fear. Gordon put his arm around him.

"Nobody will hurt you," he promised. "Tomorrow we'll find a good home for you. You can go to school and eat three meals a day, and no one will beat you. I'll be your friend."

The boy looked at him wistfully.

"I need a father," he said. "May I call you Ba-ba?"

"You may," Gordon said. "I'll look after you, and you must prove yourself by being a good son. When you are given books, you must apply yourself and learn well. Will you promise?"

"I will, Ba-ba."

They came and stood in the doorway, radiant from the fresh wind.

"Hello, Ma-ma," said the boy.

"Ah . . . hello. Come in," I said uncertainly.

When I was alone with Gordon, I asked,

"What's this Ma-ma bit? I didn't tell him to call me mother. Man! You give some people their dinner, and they invite themselves into the family. Isn't he a little speedy?"

"He's lonely," Gordon explained. "He's without parents, and he's been begging on the street for months. He's an outcast everywhere he goes. Are you going to shun him too?"

"Shunning is a strong word!" I said. "But I'd like to be asked before people call me mother. After all . . . !"

I felt the hot tears in my throat, and knew why. The woman, the defender of the nest . . . the protector of the children and the little one not yet born . . . Was this not my place, my identity? A man was an outgoing creature who could afford to be generous, but a woman must protect her nest. It was an instinct, a fighting instinct, stronger than generosity or love. That was the subtlety of it . . . it was love, but a mother love for her own, stronger than her acquired love for a world that posed danger to them. This boy was tough, he might be mean, he might be dangerous . . . Outside the home, yes . . . but under my roof, brazenly calling me Ma-ma without invitation? No!

The next day the beggar boy was settled in a children's home in the New Territories. We left new clothes for him, and soap and a comb, and some spending money. I sighed with relief. Our job was done, and he would be well cared for. It was a Christian home, and they would teach him . . .

That afternoon Gordon went to the hospital to see how the

man with the broken leg was progressing. The doctor took him aside.

"His leg will be fine," he said. "But did you know this fellow is a dope addict? He seems to want treatment for his addiction. Will you sign for him to be admitted to a treatment center?"

"If this is what he wants," Gordon said. "I'd better talk to him."

The man on the bed looked different from the haggard character on the beach. He lay between the clean white sheets, a man in his mid-thirties, with a hint of a smile in his dark eyes.

"Ah, Ding SinSaang!" he greeted. "They want to take the poison out of me!"

Gordon talked seriously with him.

"Will you work hard at this?" he asked. "You know, no one can help you unless you help yourself. You're not forty years old yet, and if you cooperate with the doctors, perhaps you can save your life from ruin. If you are discharged from the hospital cured, I'll make a promise to you. I'll help you find a job and get started over again."

The man's eyes lit up in a grateful smile, and he took Gordon's hand.

"God sent you . . ." he said. "God sent you . . ."

That evening we discussed these experiences.

"I'm beginning to think," I said confidently, "that miracles are a different sort of thing than I once imagined. Isn't it a miracle for a beggar boy to find a home . . . for a dope addict to be rehabilitated? It's almost like healing the lame or giving sight to the blind. Who says we have to pray and wait for God to stop the rain or calm the storm? To see a life changed, a man rescued from death . . . Isn't this a miracle we bring about with our own hands?"

"Maybe so," said Gordon.

I understood his reserve a few weeks later. There was a telephone call from the hospital, saying the man we found at the beach had left. After a few weeks of treatment for drugs, he had escaped, and simply disappeared, lost in Hong Kong's four million.

"He probably couldn't take it, and is back on opium," Gordon said wearily.

As if this were not enough, a month later we received a call from the children's home in the New Territories.

"The boy you brought us has run away," the voice said to Gordon. "He stole twenty dollars from the office and disappeared. Have you seen him? He seemed to think of you as his father."

We talked quietly that night, Gordon and I, puzzled by what had happened. Why had our efforts not been helpful? Didn't the man realize that he was responsible for his own future, that he had a chance to make good? How could he throw it away? Didn't the beggar boy appreciate our concern for him, our interest that he be properly cared for, even our financial assistance so that he could receive schooling and food and all the necessities of life . . . ?

I sat for a moment with my hands pressed over my eyes. How could this make sense? Under the outrage, there was a tiny working of guilt, a double-headed twinge of at once having expected much and having loved little.

I saw the boy, rushing in from the out-of-doors . . . I heard him saying bravely, Hello, Ma-ma, and there I stood, uncertain, unable to respond to him, saying, Ah . . . hello. Come in. Cordial, but oh so killing to a boy who needed love and a mother, even if for a moment.

If I did not love him, how could I expect miracles? If God was love, how could one who did not love impart anything of God, anything of the quality to be called miraculous? What we had performed were duty miracles, little utilitarian acts. We had helped, and expected a price . . . a behavior price. We had struck a cold bargain of tit for tat, and when our agreements were not kept, we felt that our efforts were in vain.

"Gordon, I couldn't love that boy . . . I didn't really care about either one of them. Do you think they felt it? How could I expect them to appreciate anything?"

"We'll learn," he said kindly. "It's easy to become possessive of those we help. Maybe we've limited God's workings to the miracles we can bring about with our own hands. Remember?"

"It's too confusing," I said. "I don't know what I'm doing."

"You're being my wife," he said.

"But what are you doing?"

"What's troubling you?"

"It seems we've chosen such a hard way to work. There are so many things to learn when you try to relate honestly to people, and you never can be sure. I guess it's the lack of sureness that frightens me. I don't mind working hard, or paring things down to the core, but how do you know when you've done it, when you've accomplished what you were trying to do? It seems that every time we set a goal it shows up as being shallow. It crumbles away, and there's another reality under it to be grasped . . . and under that there's another. When do the layers stop peeling off? How do you know when you've hit the heart of the thing?"

"I think we'll know."

"But how can we be sure? Why can't we have it written down one-two-three what we're doing? Why can't we just say the words, and leave it up to people whether they listen or not? We're not so sure of ourselves as missionaries used to be. What's wrong with us?"

"Doing things differently doesn't exactly mean we're doing them wrong," he said quietly. "I've been reading about Moses in preparation for the sermon in Chinese. Maybe Moses had this feeling. He knew there was a promised land ahead of them, yet the people all remembered Egypt more vividly because they had been there. When the difficult moments came up, they forgot how sick they had been of Egypt, and remembered only the security of their bondage. They wanted to turn back and have the sureness their fathers had . . ."

I was quiet, recalling the night of the rain and a child's indignant voice . . . *You can pray if you want, Mommy . . . I wish I could do something . . .*

Praying and doing . . . words and action . . . which of these was the real thing? Which was the servant of the other? Or was there something else, some promised land out beyond them both, of which Gordon spoke?

For the time being we had no choice. Words were important to us. It was the week of Gordon's first Cantonese sermon to an all-Chinese congregation. The fact that he was preaching in a formal service appealed to me as being something solid and above question . . . something sure.

He stood on the platform Sunday morning in his black robe, with no interpreter, and preached. The children and I sat in a back pew so we would not distract him. I listened to every tone of the now-familiar sermon, watching his face and the faces of those around me. Could they possibly know what this twenty minutes had cost him in the way of agonizing preparation? One tone could make the difference between the sublime and the ridiculous . . . Sentence after sentence the words came out of Gordon's mouth and into the ears of the people. They looked at his foreign face and heard his Chinese words. They were words about the value of work, about the necessity of using what one found in his hand and letting God bring it to life . . .

Gordon seemed relaxed as he spoke, and yet I knew it was a high point in his life. It was the culmination of days and nights of study, of dreaming in Cantonese and thinking in Cantonese, of talking to himself in the bathtub in Cantonese . . . If the intrinsic goodness of words was dubious, what good had it all done? What did it mean?

Then, as I listened, a pattern began to emerge out of his words and the faces around me. He was speaking words . . . he was talking about work . . . Was it possible that out of these two elements would come a living thing, something we could not even touch with the edge of our imagination, yet which we knew existed all along?

For some reason it sounded like a promised land. We had never seen it, but I preferred it to the security of the Fathers who knew what they were doing. What had been unquestioned sureness once might only be regression now.

The service was over. The people were gone, and Gordon took off his black robe. The Chinese pastor and the church leaders thanked him and congratulated him. He had passed the test, and was in. He had done it, had actually done it with not so much as one wrong tone.

We walked through the sanctuary to collect a few extra bulletins to keep. The long rows of pews were empty, and the church was quiet. The people were gone.

The window was open, and I leaned out over the street. Signs crowded together in jumbled profusion, and the traffic roared. The smell of garlic and ginger and steamed rice filled the air. A solid procession of people moved down the sidewalk, laughing, talking, smiling, frowning. Buses roared and street hawkers called. Across the street in a narrow passageway a young woman with a baby on her back cooked a pot of rice over an open fire. I sniffed the fragrance, overcome by a sudden impulse to go and sit beside her and taste her rice.

The church was quiet, and the people were gone.

7 THE SCHOOL

The school was built, the school we had waited for, hoped for, and driven past on Sunday afternoons. It had suddenly emerged from the scramble of bamboo scaffolding and stood, like a living thing, on the hillside. The structure climbed up the hill, following its contours so that the top laboratory section was a good dozen stories above the physical education area. It was there, with four walls to every room, waiting for some drama to take place, a drama that would eventually take on twelve hundred actors.

The first move was the selection of the players . . . the students. In order to appreciate what an occasion this was, one must know that in Hong Kong admission into a high school is very difficult. Tests must be passed, deportment checked. Entering a school is a nerve-wracking business, fraught with much tension on the part of parents and students. Rejection is as common as acceptance by reason of more students than places.

But this school, operated by the church in cooperation with the government, was classified as a private institution. It could set its own rules and proceed from there, as long as the end product could pass the government examinations upon graduation.

The day the students came to register, we had a crew of interviewers. We were instructed to look at the transcripts, ask a few questions in English (since the school was to be bi-lingual, easing toward fluency in English), and give instructions about fees and uniforms. The strangest transformation took place on faces that day. In a way, it was significant beyond the event itself . . .

A young student would come when his name was called, sit down nervously and begin to answer questions. When must he take the test? There was no test. We had checked his grades, and he would be given a chance in the new school. He could do his best, and after the first semester he would be streamed according to his own work.

"No test?" the student would say unbelievingly. "You mean there's no entrance test?"

"No, you may enter if you wish, and it's up to you to make your own standing in the school."

The incredulous look on the faces of students who were used to strenuous testing procedures was almost theological. "For everyone?" the faces said. "Oh, I'm relieved . . . I'm relieved! But what kind of a school is this? If it's for just anyone, you might get some worthless characters in here. What sort of schoolmates will I have? Don't you know I'm used to being among those who have certified their worth first?"

I had to keep reminding myself, as I sat behind a table checking applicants, that they would be tested later. They would have to prove themselves at the half-point of the year. It was too free . . . it was too easy . . . it was like proclaiming the unlimited love of God. Entrance without testing? Oh yes, fine for me, but what would become of the Kingdom of God? It wouldn't be fit to enter!

Gordon's beginning position in the school was chaplain and assistant to the headmaster. Working as a chaplain to the student body of six hundred the first year presented its own perplexity. The school, being church-related, had a chapel service every morning; yet nine-tenths of the students were non-Christian. What should be the tone of these services, held in a Christian context for an audience that was predominantly uncommitted to the Christian way?

Immediately obvious was the fact that these were not ordinary church services. They were not even like Christian college services where students come from Christian homes although the young people themselves may be uncommitted. Most of these students had no understanding of the Christian faith. To ask them to stand up and confess Christ in a creed or hymn that stated beliefs with which they did not identify was not only manipulation, it could also take the keen edge off any moment at which they might arrive in the future when these words would hopefully have meaning for them.

One decision was clear. We felt that Bible-reading in Chinese was basic to both segments. Those who had heard the words before could think about them; those who had no previous contact with the words would be hearing them. There would be no comment made for the first year on the passages read in chapel. They would be read in Chinese, then in English, and left to soak in on their own strength.

After this decision, we looked at the hymnal we had selected for the chapel services. The words were translated into Chinese so that each page was bi-lingual. This should have made it indigenous, acceptable, Chinese, fully understandable to all. But having experienced, after three years of study and work, some direction of the Chinese person's thinking, the hymns began to bother us. Into the Chinese concept of community, the hymns were speaking of separateness, of flying away from the troubles of the world and taking refuge in Christ. If the concept had clashed merely with Chineseness, perhaps we would have figured that this was the price of being Christian, and gone on with it. But many of the hymns we ourselves had grown up with now clashed with our concept of Christianness. We were in the community, seeking as Christians to be a part of the community, to feel its needs and express our love by reaching out . . . when the songs we had previously enjoyed were telling us to reach in, to come apart, to leave the world. How could we present this concept to our non-Christian students when we did not believe it ourselves? The world was already riddled with divisions and brokenness. Why contribute to this? If we had anything to share it was a faith full of trust and joy, a faith that spoke of the abundance of the spirit, a faith that was not only concerned with and involved in the life about it, but that had something valid to contribute to this life. We began making X-marks on the pages that suggested the majesty of God and the love of Jesus Christ.

In this context we began to face questions. What was the church doing in education? What were we, the representatives of the church, doing there? Asking this question, surrounded by six hundred young people, seemed ridiculous. How could a school escape being theological? Where there were people made in the likeness of God, there were automatically theological implications.

Yet the exact nature of these implications was sometimes puzzling. For every opportunity, there was a possible pitfall. In order to be honest, it was as important to be aware of the pitfalls as of the opportunities.

Particularly perplexing was the association of power, authority, and status with the name Christian. In a school where the top men were by natural order Christian, this was a distinct danger. We became aware of this one evening when a young man who had grown up in a church-related school in the East said to us, "When you are an authority, your chance to say Jesus was a nice man is washed up. You represent power, and your religion is a steppingstone to approval. I don't know about now . . .

maybe things have changed . . . but when I was in middle school the boys automatically failed after their third year if they hadn't been baptized yet. As you can see, we didn't have to be persuaded that following Jesus Christ was desirable. Religious education like this is a fear situation. You, standing in front of the classroom as a Christian, represent the authority. There is a fear that any disagreement, discussion, or question will cause bad marks . . ."

As I listened to him, I wondered . . .

Is this what has kept more Asians in a school situation from becoming Christian? Education is intended to open the mind, to send one searching for the questions beyond the questions. If religion . . . the Christian faith . . . has been presented so that it closes the mind, how can the student accept both? A person's mind cannot be both opened and closed at the same time. The only one who can do this is the person who learns to compartmentalize life . . . to have an open people-mind, and a closed God-mind . . . And in this situation God and man have no relationship. There is no confrontation and no reconciliation. Perhaps students reject this because they are mentally healthy!

To guess at the roots of a problem is relatively easy; to come up with a solution is much harder. Biblical knowledge classes were accepted by the British school system used in Hong Kong. This was a given. This was in our hands. What would we make of it?

We knew that the questions, the need if there were one, had to arise out of the culture in which these young people lived in order for the answers to have meaning. To present an arbitrary need and try to satisfy it with a foreign answer seemed to lapse back into the closed-mind circuit again. What were the needs and issues these students felt in their own lives?

Gordon took a New Testament and began reading it bi-lingually with his students. He encouraged them to talk in class, to bring up seemingly irrelevant issues, to discuss, to disagree with him. It was difficult to encourage students to disagree without destroying their native respect for a teacher.

"You must respect me as a person, and I will respect you,"

he told them. "But we have a right to disagree with each other's thinking. We have a right to question and ask and search for answers that have meaning to us about God and all of life, but we must do this in an atmosphere of mutual acceptance and trust."

The school was Gordon's place. I rarely went there except on special occasions, but we talked school night and day. There was a school song to compose, and school uniforms to design (which turned out to be a fiasco because the tailor forgot the bust darts), and there were ideas about having students come freely to our house. The problem with the latter was that they did not come. A few times on special invitation a group of students would come, but I sensed a nervousness about them that bothered me . . . both bothered and puzzled me. I had accepted them, respected them, even admired them, but there always seemed to be a question in their eyes, "What do you want from me . . . ? Why are you here . . . ? Why have you come . . . ?"

I looked at the faces, the beautiful faces with the dark eyes and the lovely black hair, and wondered if they were faces at all . . . if they were asking the questions at all, or if they were only mirrors of a kind . . . mirrors into which I looked and saw my own questions staring back at me.

What did we want? Why were we there? Would we find it in a school?

Having dared to ask the prime questions, the answer was ambiguous. If we accepted it as a purely academic situation, no. If we regarded it as a context in which human relationships could be built, a context that capsuled every ingredient of being a person, yes . . . Then, perhaps, if we remained open and acted on what our hearts taught us, we would find that elusive quality we longed for in the context of the school.

Sometimes the confidence of others made our soul-searching seem foolish. One afternoon a Chinese woman friend brought her little girl to play at the beach with our children. After swimming, the youngsters made sandwiches on our balcony, and the friend and I drank tea in the living room. I glanced out on the balcony, and saw that the Chinese child had begun to eat her sandwich first.

"Uhhh . . . you aren't supposed to eat yet," said one of our children. "We didn't pray."

"Oh, it doesn't matter," countered another. "She's not a Christian anyhow. Why should she pray?"

I winced and laughed at the same moment. When the visiting mother learned what the conversation was, she smiled and sipped her tea slowly.

"I don't know whether she's a Christian or not," she said. "My mother is a Buddhist, and I keep up the family traditions to respect her since she lives with us. But these young ones, when they go to school and hear the Bible, they have no way of separating it from the rest of their education. They think the old ways are ignorant, and want to learn the new. Who can tell? Perhaps she will be a Christian when she's a woman. These schools will turn them all into Christians!"

The optimism of her statement nearly took my breath away. She was not a Christian, and saw this as a possibility. I was one, and agonized over the possibility, not only of numbers, but of how the effect was to be achieved and what sort of results would be reaped. Would they be name-Christians . . . status-Christians . . . what-are-the-benefits Christians? Were souls being bartered for education . . . was this truly the place of the Church?

In answer there was a stirring in my mind.

The Spirit of God . . . use the words . . . do the work . . . and wait for the Spirit of God. Who do you think you are to chart the workings of God's Spirit? God was here long before you, and He will be here long after you. Shake loose . . . let go . . . raise your head and be a person, and let God move a little!

Gordon, involved in the classroom encounter and the noontime rice at the canteen, was not so abstractly troubled about these things. He was building relationships at school and enjoying the students as persons. I was just beginning to loosen up and think of the school as our parish as well. It had been established by the local church as the answer to a felt need in the society. It was a necessity, serving persons six days a week, not a Sunday morning luxury, but a daily scene of busy hands and minds, of running feet and laughing voices. It was human encounter and love expressed. Who could doubt that God was working there?

Then one morning the mail brought a letter. I read it over several times. It was from a woman in a church in the United States, the secretary of a Ladies' Guild.

". . . we have entertained foreign students in our home at various holiday times," she wrote. "They have all claimed to be Buddhists, but have attended church services with us, singing our hymns, reciting the Lord's Prayer, and discussing the Bible with us on a very impersonal basis. They admit to attending our mission schools to learn to speak better English. Are many of these students really converted?"

I laid the letter down and sighed. Would to God every bright-eyed student in the school could become a confessing, vital Christian, but was this woman aware of the complexity involved? And even beyond that, had she ever glimpsed a larger concept that even we in the situation could not comprehend . . . the concept of God's mystery and wonder and unfathomable ways?

I sat down and started to write:

". . . I begin with a firm conviction that the world is God's. It does not belong to any other power, nor is it gained for God by our efforts. God's total purposes are being worked out in all the events and ideologies of men . . ." I paused, wondering what I was saying, and how she would interpret it. "From this premise, we move to the particular society in which we live, Hong Kong. In this setting, the youth are exposed to a mass of conflicting ideas. They are the target of nationalism, communism, colonialism, traditionalism, and they have become adept at shutting their ears and looking the other way.

"In this already noisy setting, the voice of the Christian is lifted in the schools. What does it have to offer that the others are not already shouting? Equality? Communism is ahead on this. A sense of belonging in a lonely world? Nationalism can do this. Provision for physical need? Colonialism must give this in order to survive itself . . . But what does the Christian faith have to offer that the other voices do not? We would say our faith, in the life and death of Jesus Christ, offers the ultimate in love, in the respect of each individual as a person in God's sight. It says that a boy or girl is in himself valuable, is a unique being. He must not be sacrificed for mass movements nor killed in nationalistic wars nor used for profit in colonial expansion. This one individual is so important that the cross is a token of God's love for him . . . a token of reconciliation and love.

"But having stated love as the characteristic distinctive of the Christian way is self-inhibiting. Having told a person that he is valuable in God's sight, that we respect him as an individual, we cannot then turn around and manipulate him through power and advantage to accept our ideas, or dictate to him when and where he will find this reconciliation to God. We can present, can create a climate, but we cannot force. We then become only one more power in the scramble of ideologies claiming the loyalty of persons by coercion, and have destroyed our original motivation, love and reconciliation.

"When we consider the larger context of thinking in a city such as Hong Kong, and the place of the church-related school in it, we can visualize these centers as injecting Christian thinking into the bloodstream of the whole city. The other voices are there, but we are there too, and in a society where the youngsters can recite the Lord's Prayer and discuss the Bible even on a noncommittal basis, the thoughts are in their minds, in their thinking processes, and must in one way or other affect the kind of persons they will be as adults.

"You are still asking, I know, 'But what of conversion? Doesn't this woman know what simple conversion is?' Let me assure you, I do. But I can only affirm that the world is God's. His word is given, His spirit is at work. These students are unique pages on which God's message will be written, and the results may be hard for us to read. Perhaps our structures that do not fit their social patterns seem foreign to them. Perhaps some of these 90 per cent will teach us new insights about God . . . how do we know? How can we measure God's workings? We find God's workings too deep to comprehend, much less to count . . ."

I folded the letter and put it in a drawer. A few days later Gordon picked it up.

"Didn't you send this?" he asked.

"No," I answered. "I was afraid she might not understand. I'll just write her a polite letter when I'm not so churned up about it."

He laid it down, and I looked at the folded sheets lying crisply in the drawer. Perhaps what I was most afraid of was that I did not understand either . . . yet I felt the lack of understanding lay beyond both the woman's question or my answer . . . beyond what either of us knew to ask or to think. It was this very mystery of the school setting that we found totally intriguing.

8   THE COMMUNITY

The school itself was a modern white structure, but behind it on the hillside wooden huts perched like mushrooms, brownish-gray and squat. It was difficult to take a picture of the school without including this unsightly background.

One morning Gordon was walking around the school, looking at construction details. Even though classes were being held, the building crew was still adding the finishing touches, and each morning the students came to school over piles of sand and lumber. But this morning as he made his daily rounds he saw a boy playing on the sandpile. Gordon's first reaction was to call to him to get off the sandpile, and his second was to wonder why this youngster was not in school. He was no more than twelve or thirteen, a thin wiry boy with intense large eyes.

Gordon called to him, and the boy came fearfully.

"Where do you live?" he asked.

The youngster pointed up to the hillside where the little wooden houses stood.

"Aren't you in school?"

"I just finished primary school."

"Would you like to go to school here?"

The boy hung his head, and his proud eyes were hidden.

"I can't. We don't have enough money."

"What does your father do?"

"He doesn't do anything. He used to be a blocklayer, but he's very sick now."

"Does your mother work?"

The boy glanced up to where the workmen were still plastering. A small woman carried sand in baskets hung from a pole.

"That's my mother," he said.

Gordon thought for a moment. There were many things to do before noon . . . did he have time to check this out?

"Where is your father? Can I see him?" he asked.

The boy led Gordon away from the school and up the hillside to one of the tiny shacks. Inside, the father of the family lay desperately ill.

After many trips to the doctor, followed by hospitalization for major surgery, the father slowly regained his health. The boy was enrolled in the school on a scholarship, and the mother found less strenuous work. The father was eventually employed at the school. With the increased income they were able to move out of the squatter area and into better housing.

It was through this and other similar experiences that we realized the school could not be lifted out of context. It had a job to perform in itself, but was also a part of the community. The school concerns were student concerns, and the students came from families and communities. We could not understand the student except by understanding his context . . . and if we did not grasp his attitudes and unspoken thoughts, education could be only a one-way giving of facts, not a creation of meaningful relationships.

This awareness often made us think of moving into a Chinese community. We had settled in an area where predominantly foreign families, Americans and Europeans, lived. We considered this the most honest thing to do. When we came to Hong Kong we had felt foreign, and moving immediately into a Chinese community would have been disastrous. It would have been sheer martyrdom, and did not seem genuine. But that had been three years ago . . . What about now? After a total of six years in Hong Kong, three years spent working with servicemen and three years with the Chinese Church, should we still hold to this position?

We discussed this at times when we took evening walks along the beach with our children.

"You need a good home to come to, Gordon," I would say. "In school you work your head off all day . . . you give all you've got to your job. You eat rice with the students and speak Chinese all day. Don't you think you deserve a good quiet community to come home to at night? And think of the children . . . how would they feel about it?"

I looked down at my expanding waistline, and silently added, *and think of me, please . . . how much of yourself are you going to give? Is there nothing left for me?*

But Gordon's mind was moving in another direction. I felt it moving, and it made me wistful, almost afraid. One day he came back from a drive to Check Wan village and sat quietly staring into space.

"What are you thinking about?" I asked.

"I just visited Wing Sung," he said.

"Is he in trouble?"

"No . . . no, in fact, his family have just completed a new little house up on the hillside from the market. They invited us to come and see it sometime."

"That would be nice," I said vaguely. The child lay heavily these weeks, and the thought of walking through the market seemed exhausting.

"Wing Sung introduced me to an interesting boy today," he continued. "You know the woman who works at the corner vegetable stall, on the main street?"

"I think so. I can't remember."

"Wing Sung introduced me to her oldest son, Ah Yau. The two boys and I went walking through the village, and Ah Yau pointed out a hillside where there is a Communist settlement. He said to me, 'I know you don't like the Communists and they hate you Americans, but sometimes I hear them talk and what they say is good . . .' "

"He said that?"

"So I said to him, 'How do you feel when you see other families living in good houses with furniture and cars, and you have none of this?' " Gordon paused and cleared his throat and coughed. " 'I don't mind,' he said to me, 'when it's a good day and the sun is shining on everyone and I feel that I'm in harmony with the earth. But sometimes when I awake and see my mother working so hard while other women are still sleeping, and I think of how hard we try and how little we have, I wonder if there is a God anywhere, or if He is only the invention of those who want to justify their way of life. I even wonder about justice. Is it only a dream men have, or will it ever come true . . . ?' " Gordon paused, and his face was red. He was letting this thing get through to him.

"Those are strange words for a boy," I said. "How old is he?"

"Seventeen. He and his mother support the whole family. Some kids live a lot in seventeen years, if that's what you call it. They have nothing . . . absolutely nothing!"

I looked around the living room. It was modest by American standards, almost spartan. There was no rug on the floor. The curtains were made of muslin, and the furniture was second hand. Yet how must it look to a boy who slept on a wooden shelf every night . . . an intelligent, alert, highly sensitive boy who was struggling to find his place in the world?

A few days later the telephone rang.

"Ah, Ding Tai," said a young voice, "Ding Mok-si invited us to come out for a swim. Would tomorrow be all right?"

"Fine . . . *fun-ying, fun-ying!*" I said, welcoming them in my best Cantonese.

But tomorrow came, and there was another telephone call.

"We decided not to come," said the same voice. "We didn't know Ding Mok-si lived in Shallow Water Bay. If we come to your house we might be too noisy and disturb people."

I put the receiver down, feeling defeated.

There was the day we drove to Check Wan market after school. Gordon got out of the car and in a matter of seconds he was surrounded by boys and girls in the street. I heard the words, "Ding Mok-si, Ding Mok-si . . ." like birds chirruping, and saw the little hands reaching out toward him. I watched him, and wondered what his magic was. He had never given the children anything, nor bought their favor in any way.

Wing Sung came and leaned on the car window . . . I had the sensation that I had seen him standing there like this before, with that open smile on his face . . . I dismissed it, and saw Wing Sung smiling delightedly as he watched the scene in the street.

"He looks like the Pied Piper," I said laughingly. "Do you know that story?"

"No, I don't," he answered, "but I do know a story that he reminds me of. He reminds me of a story I heard about Jesus when the little children came to him . . ."

I nearly choked. Comparing us to Jesus Christ . . . How did

he have such a knowledge of the Bible? In the first place, we
were not worthy of such a comparison, and in the second place,
his comment suffocated me with a kind of unidentified personal
guilt . . . Something about his words made me want to turn on
him and say, "*You too?*" . . . and yet I did not know why his
kind comment made me so defensive. I did not even want to
know why. We were *not* Jesus Christ, and that was that. How
much did people expect of us?

It was inevitable that these workings should come to a climax
sooner or later. One evening, one of those quiet evenings when
the world seems to be coasting before it climbs the next hill, we
sat on our veranda watching as the wind swished through the
trees in front of our apartment. It was a limited view of the
world we had, only as much as the width of our apartment and
the height before the veranda upstairs cut off the green. We
seldom saw the sky, unless we went outside. It was a prescribed
view, with no unpleasantness, only well-trimmed green.

I brought Gordon a drink, and he motioned for me to sit
down.

"I've been thinking . . ." he began, "thinking a great deal.
What would you think about moving to Check Wan village?"

My heart skipped a beat, and the baby kicked. I did not reply.

"I don't feel comfortable here," he said. "Somehow the pieces
of our life aren't fitting together. What is a home for, to control
a man's life or to house it? I feel that living here is stopping me
from growing as a person, is cutting me off from expressing the
ideas I feel in my heart. It's terrible at school. The other day a
teacher asked me where we live, and when I said Shallow Water
Bay, she said, 'Oh, so you like to get away from the Chinese
after work too!' I can't tell you how that hit me . . . And you
know the choir group from the church . . . they were coming
to celebrate the moon festival with us, and then decided not to.
They might disturb the neighbors who didn't celebrate Chinese
holidays. Don't you see what we're doing? We're trying to grow
and relate and understand, and we're in a place where we can't!

Our house and our neighborhood are keeping us from building good relationships with the people we work with . . ."

He paused, and I was dully silent. To discuss a move theoretically and to consider it immediately were two different things.

"Now?" I asked.

"As soon as we can find a place."

"What next?" My voice sounded strange, desperate.

"What do you mean by that?" he asked.

"You take me out of my country and bring me to this foreign city and make me learn this godforsaken language . . . You make me see all this suffering and misery . . . and now you want me to live in a Chinese community. You want me to stop being myself! You want to destroy me as a person, and then you'll despise the old rag that is left. God knows I already don't know who I am. I see Americans walking down the street, and I hate them. I see Chinese walking down the street, and I feel like a foreign devil . . . Can't you hear me? I don't know who I am!"

Gordon looked at me.

"Be quiet," he said. "The neighbors will hear you."

"It would be a relief if someone would! And you . . . what do you think you are? What are you trying to be? Do you like going down to the village and seeing all that poverty, all that young potential squandered? It makes me sick! Of course maybe you want to live in a nice house down there, and be a big frog in a little puddle. They know we live on an American salary, and that we have enough money to live in an American community. Don't you think the condescension will show through? Just exactly what are you trying to prove?"

But Gordon was not hearing me. His eyes were dreamy . . .

"Just think of what it would be like," he said quietly. "We could rent a house . . . I already have one spotted, right in the market area, with a downstairs and a second floor. We could have a youth center for young kids like Wing Sung and his friends."

I saw myself with a little apron on, serving tea all day and all night. The children would run wild while I served as youth center hostess . . .

"What about our family?" I asked tightly.

"Oh, that could work in all right. I don't see any reason for conflict. It might be good for all of us."

"I'll tell you what would happen," I said furiously. "Our family would go to pot. You're like a man who lets his own weeds grow and goes to weed another man's garden. I actually think you would have been better off as a priest or someone who wasn't burdened with a family . . ."

He heard me. In an instant he was on his feet. There was love and anger and responsibility in his eyes.

"You're tired," he said. "If you feel that strongly about it, of course we can't do it. Whatever we do, we do together." His arm was strong and reassuring. "How many days until the baby comes now?"

"Only a couple."

I lay awake that night, squeezed by a curious fear. For all we had learned about relationships, this was too much. To accept the otherness of other people was a thing I could do . . . but to become that otherness . . . to submerge totally what I thought I was in another's style of living . . . in another's life . . . this was almost like annihilation. What if we moved to the village and I hated it, could not accept it? It would be like a soul leaving one state and not able to enter another . . . lost. The encounter was too close, the personal risk too great. Relationship? Yes, at a distance, but did I not have a right to my own identity? What motivation did Gordon have that made such a thing seem easy for him?

I lay in the darkness, afraid. The fear began to spread over me, to shake me in great convulsing pains. My mind was in such turmoil that I did not realize the pains were physical . . .

The next day, Christopher was born. I looked wonderingly at his tiny face and clutched Gordon's hand . . . and felt that somehow his birth was symbolic for all of us. He had a Chinese name and an English name, a layette and a pair of pink silk Chinese trousers that were split open at the bottom. He was our past and our future, focusing on a new point, a point between what had been and what would be. When I gazed at him the fear was gone, and my heart felt soft, like ground that had been frozen and now had melted to the spring rains . . . like ground that had been torn open by a sharp plow and now lay brown and earthy, ready for new growth to begin.

9   CHRISTMAS

It was almost Christmas again. I stood in the kitchen mixing fruit cake in a large pan. The rich batter squeezed through my fingers unheeded. It somehow did not seem so important to make fruit cake this year. I felt that it could be Christmas without it. In fact, it could be Christmas without anything . . .

I paused for a moment, perched on this feeling, and then plunged into another sensation that seemed sickeningly bottomless . . . It might not even be Christmas! For many it was not. In Hong Kong it was easy to walk down the street and around the corner on December 25 and see people who were not in any way affected. And if it was not Christmas somewhere, was it fully Christmas anywhere? Could a season like this have full meaning for anyone when it was celebrated on one street and not on another?

I wiped the dough from my hands, overcome by a sense of desolation. Christmas, a thing true on one street and unknown on another . . . It suddenly seemed arbitrary, like a questioned assumption. It was not the solid unquestioned verity for all people that I had thought it to be.

I made a cup of coffee, thinking about the nature of verity. A tormenting substance, at best, with built-in liabilities.

. . . at first we are conscious of truth as unshakable verity, and our very love of it causes us to go on searching for truth . . . and

truth leads us on and on, peering around the corners of our minds. We tramp and tramp, and truth comes to us in snatches of light like the pinpoint exposure of a film. And suddenly we collect the exposures and develop them and the picture does not portray what we originally held as verity. We are far from what we at one time considered the unquestioned picture of truth . . . and this new exposure frightens us. We want to throw away the film, to destroy the evidence and turn back . . . but there is no turning back. The new picture is indelible in the mind. To return voluntarily to what one once considered an absolute is in itself a contradiction. One does not choose absolutes, they are thrust upon us . . . When we choose to return to a one-time absolute, it can only be for one of two reasons: a regression out of fear, or a conscious choice, neither of which is the same as an unquestioned assumption . . . a verity.

I filled the pans with dough and put them in the oven, then went to check on the baby. He lay like an early gift in his bed, sleeping blissfully. I glanced at my watch. The children would soon be home from the school play rehearsal, and Gordon would be late tonight. Christmas was a busy time of year. Perhaps I would get caught up in the busyness and catch the spirit hindside to. I hoped so. All that work with no meaning would be unbearable . . . not that there was no meaning, but what the meaning was no longer seemed so crystal clear . . . so easy to express in a few succinct words. It was there, waiting to take form, felt but undefined, true but not unchallenged, under the surface but wary of its own expression.

The weather had turned cold, cold for Hong Kong. I breathed in the spicy air and romped with the older children, hoping that perhaps this would bring on the yuletide feeling. We hung pine branches in our living room, and I made a life-size chalk drawing of Mary with the baby Jesus in her arms. We hung this up as well, and somehow I felt centered in. If only I could gaze at that picture and comprehend what I had expressed with my own hands, perhaps it would come. Every time I passed the drawing it seemed like a gift still in the wrapping, only it was my spirit that was wrapped, covered over with some substance that made it impervious to the meaning of the picture.

The cakes were baked and the greens were hung. The children were decorating the tree the night we realized we wanted to have the party, the party that was to make this Christmas memorable . . .

"When we finish the tree let's drive to Check Wan and invite Wing Sung and his friend Ah Yau who walked with me that day," Gordon suggested, "and perhaps anyone else they would like to bring along."

"What date shall we invite them for?" I asked.

"We'll have to check first to see when they'd be free."

We bundled up the children, piled into our mini-car, and chugged around the corners and over the hills to the south side of the island.

The market in cold weather had taken on a changed look. Gone was the carefree air of outdoor living. Men and women wore silk padded jackets, and hunched against the sharp wind from the sea. The open-air restaurant on the corner was a pillar of steam holding its own against the icy air. Even the dogs along the street looked colder and hungrier and more worried . . . The market was fastened in on its own life, fighting to survive until the warm winds of spring would unfold it.

We searched for Wing Sung in the fish stall, but he was not there. A woman directed us to the noodle stall, where we found him sitting on a rough wooden stool, consuming a bowl of hot stringy noodles in a small cloud of steam.

"Ah, Ding Mok-si!" he said through the noodles.

"Eat slowly . . . eat slowly . . ." Gordon greeted him in Cantonese.

The other customers stared curiously as we arranged a date with Wing Sung.

When the party was set, we had invited Wing Sung and his family, at least as many as could come, Hoh, the boy who

of Christmas. They knew that Jesus Christ had been born and that we were celebrating his birth, but what was he to them? Wing Sung had said, "She knows a lot of foreign things . . ." Was there some way this Christ could be more to them than the Lord of foreign things . . . could be known as one who walked the streets of Check Wan market?

I remember the rice that night, and the beautiful young faces softened by candlelight . . . and the face of the Christ-child over the table, and Gordon's face, and the faces of our children. We moved closer together, and the extra place at the table seemed to have been taken. There were no spaces or gaps and we were not crowded . . .

We tried the fruit cake, and the teenage girl said, "Not too bad. It tastes a little like moon cake, but too sweet."

We played a game and used Chinese numbers, and the Chinese children won . . . We played it with Western numbers, and our children won . . .

We played a game of "bomb," a windup device that ticked, then popped on one person's lap with a forfeit to be paid. We tossed it with great gusto, laughing as though there were no neighbors . . . Then it landed on the little girl and exploded in her lap. She covered her face in shyness, and I suddenly felt overcome. The girl was real and the bomb was real, and when she took her hands away there would be no face. This was what was happening between Asians and Americans not many miles away . . . and we wondered why Christmas had a hard time meaning what it should.

I walked into the kitchen to get a drink, my whole body shivering. How could we talk about Christmas in a world where men did not know the meaning of reconciliation?

It was time for them to go back to Check Wan on the bus. The little girl came with Wing Sung to say thank you.

"Now can you sing for us?" we asked.

She looked at Wing Sung, who nodded his approval. Mustering her courage, she sang the Chinese words in a tiny voice:

Yuhn yuhn joih ma-cho leuih . . . *far away in a manger,*
No pillow and no bed,
Little Lord Jesus slept very peacefully and well.
And the stars also gazed down at his sleeping place . . .
Little Lord Jesus, sleeping on the dry grass.

My God, I thought, *she's even expressing it in Chinese, and still thinks of it as a foreign thing. What does it take to make it hers?*

After the guests were gone and the children were asleep, Gordon and I sat by the little electric fireplace in the living room, surrounded by a strange uneasiness. It was as though the two of us were not really alone . . . as though a presence enveloped us, a presence that at once drew us together and stood between us.

I glanced instinctively at the picture above the table. The flickering candle, now burned low, was giving an odd illusion of movement to the faces . . . I stared at them, fascinated. The incarnation . . . God among us . . . What did it mean? What did it mean in this life situation?

There was a twisting, like pain, like a heel grinding seeds into the plowed earth of my heart . . .

Could it be? Could this be it? Was this the word my mind had been longing for and resisting at the same time . . . the word it had been reaching for and fighting against? The word . . . the Word become flesh and living among us, not in the next town where conditions were better, not in an occasional visit to say hello and then retreat . . . not with an invitation for a holiday, but among us. He had come to live in a place like the village, among people who knew the sting of daily physical hardship . . . He had come to share every part of their existence until they knew their questions about God and their questions about life were one. He had not been afraid to lose his identity in the bringing about of reconciliation!

I turned to Gordon and at the same moment he held out his hands, sensing my thoughts.

"Would you like to . . ." he said, "to live in the village?"

"When?" I asked. "Tomorrow?"

He laughed and clasped me tightly and I cried and he cried, and we wiped each other's tears . . . and sat watching the candle burn down to a sputtering stub while we talked quietly . . .

This thing called incarnation . . . It keeps growing on us. It swells up in us and we must become larger or it kills us . . . How else can we contain it? The facts never change . . . the baby in the manger, the man on the cross . . . but the meaning grows and reaches in and unsettles us and pushes us into new and frightening situations that threaten to destroy us . . . and make us cry out for the living God. How else can we bear it?

"Is this what made all those difficult things easy for you?" I asked Gordon. "Why didn't you come out and tell me?"

"How can you tell anybody?" he replied.

And I understood. It was not a thing that one could turn around and proclaim, "Look! I have it!" It was more the glimpsing of a glory that could lead one on and on, transfixed . . . a moving, living verity that affirmed itself with its own realizations, a truth that could accept discovery and not be destroyed.

Christmas was an unpredictable thing, a different thing each year. This year it seemed to be a beginning, a promise. Suddenly, I could believe that it was Christmas everywhere, whether men celebrated it or not.

"Next year we're going to light a candle on the village main street and put it in the window," I said. "A bright red candle, for happiness."

10   WITH DUE RESPECT

It was Chinese New Year. Red firecracker papers lined the streets, and families walked about in their New Year finery. Everyone had at least three days off, for some the only holiday all year. Each day had its special significance, its proper relative to visit, its correct meal to serve. Small bundles of oranges in string bags were carried from house to house, and tea was served to every guest, accompanied by lotus seeds, sweet coconut, and candied vegetables. Everywhere children greeted their elders with *Gung hei faat choi*, wishing them happiness and prosperity in hope of a red packet containing lucky money.

In Check Wan village, the streets were gay with bright colors. The fishing boats were parked in the harbor, festooned with red papers wishing the inhabitants good luck in the new year.

One morning during the week-long festival, we walked through the market with our children. Gordon had spotted a

house he wanted us to see. The house was a rather tall thin crackerbox of a building with three small floors, but the location was its selling point. It faced the sea on one side, where the fishing boats came in each morning. Across the street was the Chinese rice-wine brewery, and to the left of the house stood a huge banyan tree with joss sticks burning under it. The doorstep was only three or four feet from the street, and the street was used by everyone in town. If we wanted to be in the middle of things, this was certainly the house for us!

A few days after we decided to rent the house by the sea, Wing Sung came to visit us. For some reason he was not his usual friendly, relaxed self. I served him tea and a tray of Chinese New Year delicacies, then waited for whatever was troubling him to come to the surface. After a few minutes of polite talk, he bit into a piece of sweetened coconut and looked at it with unwarranted concentration.

"Most Westerners don't serve this at New Year," he said. "Who taught you to buy it?"

"A friend."

He stared at the ceiling, then at the curtains, then at the floor.

"This house is very nice," he said finally.

"It has been a good place to live."

"This neighborhood is considered to be very high class," he said.

"There are many good people here," I assured him.

There was an uneasy silence. He picked up his teacup, then set it down abruptly.

"Why are you moving into our village?"

His tone made me wary of too quick an answer.

"Why do you think we are?" I countered.

He dropped his eyes, a slow blush stealing over his face.

"It would be hard for you to hear," he said quietly.

"One must always be ready to hear the truth," I said.

"Then you must not think me disrespectful. I only tell you because you asked. According to my way of thinking, when you live here with the other foreigners you must feel it is a waste of your time. When you speak to them about your religion, they don't have to listen. They have money, and can go out to the theater and forget what you have said. But in our village, it is different. We're poor people, and will listen to you because we have few amusements. At night when our work is done, what you have said will stay in our minds, and slowly we will all begin to believe what you say."

"How will we do this?" I asked, fascinated.

"You'll hold meetings in your house and give the children toys and candy, and pass out little papers for them to take home to their parents. You'll promise us heaven if we listen to you and hell if we don't . . . and slowly you'll turn us all into Christians."

His voice remained quiet, but his eyes were angry. I sat stunned for a moment. What we saw as an opportunity, Wing Sung saw as exploitation . . . exploitation of his friendship. What we wanted to give, he was afraid was going to get him. How could we be true to our Christian motivation of sharing the love of God as revealed in Jesus Christ, and yet show this boy that we respected him first of all as a person . . . as the person he was at that moment, and not the person he might become if he someday conformed to our thinking?

I groped desperately for an answer, and one came.

"Wing Sung, when we move to your village, we ask you to teach us. We want to know more about the things you say and do, about your life. How can we learn that here? We feel our lives will be more meaningful if we share them with you in your village. We want to learn . . . do you believe that?"

"Perhaps," he said doubtfully.

"Will you believe just one thing?"

"What thing?"

"That we want to be your friend whether you ever become a Christian or not?"

He looked at me uncertainly.

"Perhaps I can, since I know you," he said, "but usually it would not be so. My brothers and the people in the village will never believe it, not until they see it."

It was like being in a trance . . . like having one's fortune told.

"What else should we know?" I asked quietly. "What will be the most important thing to remember?"

A look of pain crossed his tan face.

"Remember not to look down on people," he said simply.

After Wing Sung left, I sat staring into space, dumfounded. For him to have spoken in this manner was a genuine token of friendship, yet to realize that the acceptance of our family in his village was as much a threat to him as it had been to me was a revelation. The range was too close for any of us to remain as we were, and the thought of becoming like the other was frightening. The breaking down of a final barrier left us all awash in each other's territory, in each other's lives. Would we be lost without barriers?

When Gordon came home from work, we discussed the problem. How would we relate to the people in the market? From Wing Sung's warning it was obvious that formal services on Sunday would meet with deaf-eared resistance and weary hostility. The village people had had this experience somehow, somewhere.

"How about Saturday nights?" Gordon suggested. "Could we have open house and snacks and records, and let the young people come and organize their own parties?"

"I don't know. We'll have to wait and see what the whole feeling is. Some conservative Chinese parents might be aghast at the idea of a Saturday night party. We don't want to go overboard the other way and shock people."

"No . . . Come to think of it," Gordon said, "why must we do anything? Why do we feel we have to move into a town and organize the place? Can't we just be a family on the corner with an open door and a friendly smile? Why don't we just live in the market as a Christian family, and see what happens?"

"That sounds best," I agreed. "We have our formal responsibility at the school. Perhaps at home we could experiment in a new kind of unstructured relationships."

In spite of any misgivings they might have had about our coming, the people of Check Wan gave us a royal welcome.

The day we moved was unforgettable. Packing boxes and people, children and toys, bedding and cups of tea, were mixed through each other on the ground floor. Up the winding stairway there were children, ours and their new friends, playing hide-and-seek in the unplaced furniture. I walked up to the third level to find a moment of quiet, and instead found two little boys flying a kite out of the bedroom window. We wanted to make friends, and by all appearances we certainly had succeeded!

They were wonderful friends from the start. One woman brought a bucket of freshly laid eggs, and another a bag of oranges. Wing Sung and his friend Ah Yau unpacked and washed the dishes. Someone's younger brother helped set up the beds . . . and just about dark when we began to wonder how we could possibly prepare a meal in this confusion, Wing Sung's mother, Wong Tai, came to the door, gathered our children, and took them to her house on the hillside for dinner. We had found good neighbors as well as friends.

It was strange, once we had moved to the village . . . the poverty did not seem so poor. Instead of seeing the rickety furniture and the old pails in which people did their wash, I noticed the smile in eyes and the enthusiasm people had for living. There was a contentedness to be, and the objective was existence. It struck me as being a singularly rich kind of life, poor only in the things that others thought necessary. I found myself trying to simplify, not because I pitied people, but because I envied them.

Once the house by the sea was settled, we resumed our routine. Gordon went to the school every day, and the children attended the British Government school. Baby Christopher and I kept house. At night we all came together and enjoyed the village. The children in particular began to explore every street and alley. Young Michael was in his glory.

"Dad . . . Mom . . . you know what I found?" he said one day. "I found a shop where they have jars of wine with snakes in them . . . real live snakes!"

"Live?" I quizzed.

"Well . . . they used to be . . ." he corrected sheepishly, and I felt guilty of killing both the snakes and his enthusiasm.

And Chinese words, which we had never been able to induce them to learn, suddenly took on new interest for them. The customary pieces of paper in Michael's jeans were now scribbled with his private spellings of Chinese words. "That's my vocabulary list," he explained. "I know over thirty words now. Wing Sung is teaching me when I go up to his house to help him cook."

The girls made friends with Wing Sung's sister, Mei Ho, and she often played at our house. One day when it was time for dinner, I said,

"Mei Ho, we're going to eat soon. It's almost dark . . . don't you think your mother will be wondering where you are?"

She pouted her small lips, looked at me in surprise, and walked slowly out of the door.

The next day our children were playing at Mei Ho's house. When they came home, they had already eaten lunch. The next time I saw Wing Sung I thanked him.

"That was good of your mother," I said. "I didn't expect her to keep them for lunch."

"We never send people away when we're getting ready to eat," he said simply, and I got the message. After that, neither did we. I began to put an extra potato or scoop of rice in the pot, and if anyone was around, we invited him to eat with us. But in some things we did not want to change. No matter how many guests were present or who they were, we carried out our family habits as usual, reading from the Bible and having prayer at the table. These things we did for our own sake, and did not consider them as directed toward others but simply shared, as we shared our food.

At night when the market was closed and the village chores were done, the young people began to come in, Wing Sung and Ah Yau with two or three of their friends. At times teenagers from the school and the Brotherly Love Church came and mixed with the youngsters from the village. We began to have a feeling of integrity, of the integration of all the parts of our life . . . and the quantity of what happened became increasingly less important than the quality. We were content to provide an atmosphere and let the young people talk . . . and as they talked we began to learn the temper and nature of this group with whom we had chosen to work. On the whole, they were much the same as teenagers in the United States, yet in some ways they were more naïve, in others, more sophisticated. On the subject of girls, we found Chinese boys less vocal than Americans. A boy of sixteen or seventeen still considered himself a child; he had a healthy admiration for the opposite sex, but was seldom in a binding relationship to any one person. Boy-girl relationships were for the most part carried out in the "group," with group activities such as swimming, hiking, and picnicking seeming to satisfy the need for social contact without throwing the young people into a one-to-one relationship. Courtship and marriage were considered a grave responsibility, not to be fallen into lightly or too young.

Sometimes the subject of religion would come up and we would listen. What were they saying? The young people from the Brotherly Love Church were stanch Christians, and they never hesitated to say so. The school group was of mixed opinion. Most of the village youth were Buddhists or chose not to believe anything, at least not consciously. Wing Sung was vocal in this matter. One day when I was on my way up the stairs, I heard his voice coming from the living room.

"My grandmother was a Buddhist, and my mother is, and I suppose you could call me one too, as far as my family goes. But in my heart I have difficulty believing as they do. So many of the beliefs seem old and dark and loaded with superstition . . ."

"Ah, they will make a Christian of you yet!" a girl said with a laugh.

"Not so fast," came Wing Sung's voice. I paused on the winding stairway to hear his answer. "If there's anything I don't like, it's to hear someone else make fun of my parents' faith. Perhaps it isn't mine, yet I must respect it as I respect them."

"It's better to be a Christian now," said the girl.

"Why do you say that?"

"My mother says the educated people are becoming Christians. The traditional religions are becoming old-fashioned."

"Hah, you women," Wing Sung retorted. "Is God a fashion, or religion a style that you change like you change your dress? What was true is always true. Truth does not go out of style. One thing you must watch is following something because it is in fashion, or because it will bring you some benefit like social standing or a place in the Christian cemetery to be buried. When people believe for what they can gain by it, how can it be a belief of the heart?"

"Then you still follow your parents?"

"No . . . I do not. But neither will I follow a thing that I do not yet understand. It is the superstition in the traditional religion that seems untrue to me . . . yet who can say that the Christian way is free of it? A man, born without a father . . . a dead man coming to life . . . Are these natural stories? Sometimes I think I can as easily believe our own supernatural tales as these. If I ever become a Christian it will be because I see Christians are good men. One must watch and evaluate and follow the best . . ."

Gordon brought a guitar into the living room, and it was eagerly taken by young hands. I turned on the water for tea and fixed the cookie plate, my ears ringing from the conversation. At that moment, cookies and tea did not seem like drudgery, but like a small price to pay for being tuned in on where these youngsters stood in their own world. In my mind's eye I arranged them all in orderly rows in church, and smiled to myself. Who would ever have heard that conversation in church?

It was the moon and the day for the festival of Tin Hau, goddess of the sea. This was an important event for the people of Check Wan, especially the fishermen. Tin Hau had the power to insure a good catch of fish, protection from the sharks, and good luck for the boat people. It was most necessary that her favor be invoked.

We had seen signs of the coming event being assembled in the market for over a week. In front of the fish stall, a large rectangular frame was covered with bright pieces of paper until it looked like a float.

Now this morning, this moon and this day, all was ready. We

heard the sound of the drums coming down the market street, and stood out on the sidewalk in the crowd by our door to watch the procession.

"Should you get your camera?" I asked Gordon.

"No," he said quietly. "It will make us outsiders."

"As if we aren't already," I retorted softly. I looked around us at the crowd gathering on the street. We were the only ones with faces like ours . . . non-Chinese faces. I felt included and fortunate and excluded and unfortunate all at once . . . With a sense of shock I realized any previous image I had of myself was gone, and with it my whole prerogative to judge. I was merely a spectator, taking in what was going on, nondirective, noncritical. I was like a plant on the sidewalk, growing out between a crack in the cement . . .

The drums were beating, like a giant communal heart. I felt my own heartbeat quicken, out of step with the pulsation in the air . . . felt it race ahead, then slow again until the beating of the drums and the thumping of my heart were synchronized . . . as though my heart had left its own rhythm and was following the vibrations around it . . .

The crowd surged down the street. In the center of the crowd four men carried the float on poles featuring an image of the sea goddess. There was a whole roast pig with an apple in its mouth and a display of fruit.

The drums were beating, now accompanied by the sound of chanting voices. Along the edge of the crowd boys and young men carried flags and banners.

Gordon nudged me. "Look, there's Wing Sung."

He was marching with the flag-bearers. We waved to him, but he nodded quickly and turned away as though he wished we had not seen him.

The drums pounded and the chanters chanted, and the procession moved on past our house and down the street to the temple and the sea.

When it was dark that night and the children had had their last drink of water and were asleep, there was a knock at the door. It was Wing Sung. In his hands he held a plate of pork sliced from the processional pig.

"My mother sent this," he said shyly.

"How thoughtful of her!" I said, accepting the plate with both hands. "Your mother has a good heart. Come in and sit awhile."

He stood painfully at the door, his head down and his hands behind him.

"You must be very angry with me," he said.

"Why should we be angry?"

"Because you don't believe in Tin Hau."

"You don't have to live by what we believe, do you?"

He raised his eyes and stared first at Gordon, then at me, in surprise.

"No," he said at last. "Perhaps I'm blaming you for my own feelings. I don't believe in this festival myself . . . and when you looked at me, I couldn't bear to face you. I didn't want to march today, but someone put a flag in my hand, and I carried it . . ."

He slumped against the doorframe, dejected.

"Do Christians ever do that?" he asked. "Do they ever get swept along with the crowd, or do they practice only the customs they honestly believe in?"

He was standing in a doorway, lost from one identity and unsure of the next . . . and he and we were one.

Gordon put his arm around the boy's shoulders, and we talked for a long time, talked about carrying flags that are put in our hands . . . about carrying them simply to avoid trouble instead of to express faith.

When Wing Sung left, he seemed like a younger brother. If we could meet in our lostness, we culturally and he religiously, perhaps we could someday meet in our foundness.

It was a lonely night, a sad night in a way, yet the swish of the waves on the beach across the road seemed to whisper something. I listened for some promise, some word of hope. Perhaps it was good for one to be lost in some area, for how could the totally found have any empathy with those who were searching? Perhaps partial lostness was the state of those who chose to live without barriers. Inside a small familiar fence, one could feel secure . . . but in a wide-open world with a bare heart, how could one ever feel concluded?

11 EXPECT THE UNEXPECTED

I poured rice into the pan and washed it with care, then added just enough water so that my hand, spread out over the rice, was submerged. While the rice was steaming I picked up a straw basket and went around the corner to buy some fresh vegetables in the market.

At the vegetable stall, Yau Tai was expansively friendly.

"Ah, Ding Tai, don't take those beans. Those are from yesterday. Here . . . these are fresher."

"Ah, Yau Tai, you have such a good heart. You shouldn't be so polite."

"Ah, who is so polite? My son said he had a good time at your house last night . . ."

She talked on in the deep earthy voice of the market women while I looked over the cucumbers. How different this was from shopping in a supermarket! Supermarket? I had hardly thought of the word for months. What would I do if I ever walked down an aisle again, pushing a cart? The whole idea of all that variety seemed ridiculous. If one had a little rice and vegetable, and a few kinds of meat or fish, what more could one want?

Dinner was almost ready when there was a knock at the door. I opened it to see Ah Chun, the short round shoeman, and his two tiny daughters. He looked like a distraught father who had been sent with the children to get them out of mamma's hair.

"Ah Chun! How did you ever find our new home?"

"Ah, Ding Tai, I know where you are. It's good to come here, just like a Chinese house. I even smell rice cooking."

"So it is. Won't you and your daughters come in to stay and have rice with us tonight?"

"No, no . . . it would trouble you."

"No, no! We would be honored."

"You shouldn't be so polite. Very well, just a bite. We must not stay long, we don't want to trouble you."

"Come in and sit . . ." I went to get hot tea for him, and left the little girls to get acquainted with our children while I pre-

pared the meal. I heard the *put-put* of the mini-car against the curb, and knew Gordon was home.

It was only a simple meal of rice and meat, with greens from Yau Tai's stall, but it will always stand out in our minds as a most significant occasion. We gathered around the table, held hands as a family and friends, and Gordon thanked God for the food in Chinese . . . then Michael repeated the prayer in English. Just as we were ready to raise our heads, Ah Chun began to speak. I looked at him, and realized his eyes were closed and his head was bowed. I closed my eyes and listened. He was speaking to God in a prayer that made my heart stand still. He prayed in Jesus' name, a prayer direct and simple. It was silent for a moment.

"Ah Chun!" Gordon said, extending his hand. "I didn't know you were a Christian!"

"Ding Mok-si! I didn't either! I wasn't, but I am! This is the first time I've ever prayed aloud to God . . . the first time! You were all praying, and I felt my heart move and tell me to pray. I've prayed to God aloud for the first time!"

I sat with head down, not daring to look up. To hear a man establishing a speaking relationship with God was an awesome thing . . . an awesome thing to happen over rice and tea and half-washed hands, clasped in a squirming circle of peeping children and tired adults at the end of a day. Did awesome things happen in this way?

I cleared the dishes, picking up the chopsticks and brushing up the rice, and feeling as if there were twelve basketsful left over. Was this how the disciples had felt when they brought their five loaves and two fishes to Jesus, and organized the crowd, and passed out the food, and collected up the remains? Yes, I could feel it now. They were almost finished before it hit them. Five loaves and five thousand people? How could that be? What a gap between what was and what happened. There must have been a miracle!

I walked to the kitchen in a daze. A miracle . . . what was a miracle? Its meaning seemed to be constantly changing, unfolding. There was a time when I thought a miracle to be something cosmic, like stopping a storm or the rain, until that definition proved unreliable. And then I thought we had to arrange God's miracles for Him, and all He had to do was to supply the electricity, like changing dope addicts or lives that in our opinion were not being properly lived . . . But this, this happening of tonight, was not of our planning. It had come through us, but not of us. It had taken place in our context, helped by our words, warmed by our work, but certainly catapulting us into a sense of wonder that we had never anticipated nor would have known how to bring about. It was the wonder of God's doing. Was this not miracle in its truest form?

In the days that followed, new definitions began to come to mind. Questions such as "What is mission?" and "Why identify?" now seemed to merge into a single pattern and be parts of a whole. Now I saw mission as the building of bridges, bridges between God and man, yes, but between man and man as well. The world seemed at once welded in God and fragmented by men, and the Christian word became the word to heal the fragmentation. And mysteriously, when the barriers between men came down, there was a contact living and vital between them in which the presence of God was discovered. Relationships between man and man became an integral part of discovering God.

In this new context, identification was a different word. Identification was inward, a touching of heart to heart, oblivious of external signs. To wear a Chinese dress was good, but it was just as good to wear Western clothes. To eat rice was good, but to prepare a Western meal to share was sharing on the same level. To have a house when some had none was still painful, but to leave the door open to all who would enter was to have a place to contain relationships. It was not our house. It was a place to build bridges, to relate, to share the love of God with all for whom it was intended.

And at last I began to understand what "Share the love of God" meant. It had none of the connotation that we brought this love to hand out to others . . . that was a gross assumption.

It meant that they and we were mutual sharers of a great bond that reached out to all, a great proclamation that included us all . . .

You have been accepted. Do not fear the anger of God or the hostility of men . . . they are both of your own making. Tear down your ancient walls and throw away your fears. God is among you. God loves you!

In fact, the tide was sometimes reversed, and we became the recipients of insights from our Chinese friends. They shared the love of God with us. There was Fong Tai, the mother of many sons, who came each Saturday to chat with us and show us tricks of Chinese cooking. She sat patiently and taught me how the women think and feel about life in Hong Kong, and what some of the sayings are in which these feelings are expressed.

"A garment made by a mother is like covering a child with his mother's love," she taught me one day. And although she was not his mother, she knit a warm sweater-suit for baby Christopher. It was she who taught us to wash our hands in tea after eating seafood, and to squash garlic buds in the proper way to bring out the best flavor. She shared of her warm heart and friendly spirit until I could not imagine there had been a time when we did not know her. Somehow, in the love of God, we always had.

There was the memorable evening when Geen Sun and his girlfriend Lilly came to tell us of their engagement. They were two young people from the Brotherly Love Church and had been in the group Gordon taught during his language school months. Now they had decided to marry, even though the girl's mother disapproved. The day of strictly parent-approved marriages was disappearing, and the young people had more choice in marrying a mate of their own liking.

We received the news with handshakes and hugs and good wishes all around for a hundred years of happiness and many sons, then settled down to an evening together.

As we talked with them, Gordon asked,

"Geen Sun, there's a song I've heard you sing in Chinese Church that has such a beautiful tune. I wonder if you'd know it by heart?"

"How does it go?"

"I can hardly remember. All I know is that it's a Chinese tune."

"Could it be *Tin sung dik Fuh-Chun*?"

"I don't remember the words, just the tune."

Geen Sun hummed the tune, and we both recognized it instantly as one we had heard Chinese Christians sing with fervor. But the words, being in classical Chinese, had escaped us.

"Can you translate the lines into conversational Chinese?" Gordon asked.

"I'll try," he said obligingly.

We worked for several hours, first learning the classical characters and their meaning, then translating the song into English. When we were finished, we sang it over and over, reveling in the verse sung to an old Buddhist tune.

> *My merciful heavenly Father*
> *Who day by day sustains my life,*
> *I ought to obey Him,*
> *Bow humbly before Him.*
> *He's the Spring Wind,*
> *I am the grass.*
> *Let Him blow.*

Long after Geen Sun and Lilly had left, we sat humming the enchanting tune and discussing the meaning of the words.

"In a way," Geen Sun had said, "this song is more significant to us than some that have been translated from the English, because it expresses our feeling of the inferior and the proper attitude toward the superior. All men are as grass, and when God, the great wind, blows, who can stand before Him? Can the grass hold up its head before the wind?"

There was a new perspective gained with learning this song. Relationships between man and man were not an arbitrary thing. We were by nature related. All men were as grass . . . and how could one grassblade relate itself to the wind without stirring the others? It was an impossibility. God, like the wind, was both among men and transcendent over them, and one man could no more raise his head and find God alone than one blade of grass alone could be stirred by the wind. The movement of each moved the other, and God was the prime mover. God . . . man . . . the above and the within . . . the wind in the grass.

Was this only Chinese, or had we heard it before?

> *As for man, his days are as grass:*
> *As a flower of the field, so he flourisheth.*
> *The wind passeth over it, and it is gone,*
> *And the place thereof shall know it no more.*
> *But the mercy of the Lord is from everlasting . . .*

The Spring Wind!

He's the Spring Wind, I am the grass . . . A revelation, yet deeply echoed in our own taproots.

Riding high on the crest of this discovery, we welcomed the visit of Mrs. Lee one afternoon. She came in, looked around our house, and nodded to herself, her black eyes perceptive as ever.

"You missionaries are an odd lot," she said with a smile. "Each one a rebel in his own right."

"How are the other students doing?" Gordon asked. "I've often wondered about the priest—what was his name? Schaperelli? Where is he now?"

"Do you mean the one who was always asking shocking questions? He's lost himself in a resettlement area parish, and is raising eyebrows now by pushing birth control. I asked him the other day if he were still concerned about saving the heathen from hell, and he said, 'You bet I am . . . and ten kids is my description of hell!' "

We chuckled together over the outrageous young priest, then remembered others who had been in the class.

"What about Porter?" I asked.

"In what regard?" Mrs. Lee probed.

"What is he doing?"

"I don't know what Mr. Porter is doing. All I know is that he and his family have gone back to the States. You know, he never developed an interest in the people here as such, and I think the language was an impossibility as a result. Language is a people-oriented art, and only those who have a genuine interest in people for people's sake seem to master it. I've seen several of these strictly God-oriented missionaries pack up and go home . . . and more of them who should, but who haven't got the courage."

"Why do you say that?" I asked defensively.

"I feel sorry for this type of person," she said slowly. "He firmly believes that the mass of the Chinese are on their way to destruction, yet his hostility toward us makes it impossible for him to relate or communicate, and he can only torment himself with his own belief. The higher his conviction rises, the more his anxiety cuts him off from other people until he becomes an alienated person almost eager for the judgment of God to avenge his own suffering . . . like Jonah under the vine."

I watched her, tiny, delicate, sipping her cup of jasmine tea, yet with a mind like a mowing machine cutting relentlessly at whatever came across her path. Her direct attack on someone I had thought to be at least sincere embarrassed me, yet I felt a moment of relief that she was castigating someone beside us for a change. Did not the fact that she was pointing out someone else's failure indicate that she thought we were doing better?

When she had gone, I gathered up the teacups with an uneasy feeling in the pit of my conscience, an undefined guilt that erased the joyous freedom of the previous days.

We talked about Porter that evening, and I realized that I had almost rejoiced in his defeat . . . had built a wall around him as someone who deserved failure . . . and I myself was on the other side of that wall.

O God! How many walls do we have within our walls? When the walls are broken down between us and our created brothers, and we find ourselves behind walls of scorn for our Christian brothers, what have we gained?

O God! Free us from the walls within the walls. Free us from the walls where we want to stand and shout victory when our very shouting sounds like the cock's crowing.

O God! Make us free . . . free like the grass to bend with the wind, with no consciousness of our rightness or wrongness, but only of your greatness.

The next day Mrs. Lee telephoned, and I talked to her with mixed feelings. Who was this woman, this self-appointed angel of enlightenment? Her words had tremendous weight, and yet they usually succeeded in making me thoroughly angry.

Her voice was quiet over the wire, and the connection was bad, blurring out several times during the conversation.

"Excuse me, I can't hear you," I said.

Her voice was clear for a moment.

"I was saying there's one more thing I would like to tell you and Gordon to be aware of . . . one thing I've hesitated to tell you until now, but which I think you're ready for at this point . . ."

Her voice faded and there was a hum.

"Yes?" I said eagerly. "Hello . . . hello?"

Only the hum of the wires answered.

I stood, holding the dead phone, when there was a knock at the door. I opened the door and there stood the beggar boy, brown and ragged and dirty as the day Gordon found him.

"Ma-ma," he said in his husky voice.

I laid the phone down quickly and put my arms around him and gave him a squeeze. I did not know what the future held for him, but that did not matter now. I would not let this moment pass unheeded again.

Perhaps life in relationships would be like this . . . an insight here, a broken connection there, and even a chance to do some things over again. It was no easy task. How could one ever learn to be a person under heaven?

12   THE SPRING WIND

For almost a week the spring opera had been on in Check Wan. It was the last night of the performance, and Wing Sung's family had invited us. There was no set time for the program to begin, and no one seemed to know when it would end, except that it would be late.

It was almost dark when our family walked with Wing Sung and his sister Mei Ho to the opera house, down along the sea. Already we could hear the *clang, clang-clang* of the opera instruments and the high wailing pitch of the singer.

The opera house was a large rough structure, put up temporarily for the season each year. To leave it up during the typhoon season would be disastrous, for the severe sea winds would rip it to shreds. It was open on all sides, with a domed roof constructed of bamboo poles and thatched with rattan mats. On the stage actors with lavish costumes and heavily painted faces came out to sing their bits, while the crowd milled in and out at will, drinking soda pop or soybean milk, and exchanging the village gossip.

The few chairs available were taken when we came, and we stood, elbow to elbow with the crowd, drinking soda pop from bottles splashed with Chinese characters. The music was strange to me, but I began to feel that it was folk music, the stories of people and their loves and fears, of their wars and victories . . . people singing the songs of their past in order to reassure themselves that they were, and that they would be. A woman behind me bumped me and did not say excuse me, and for the first time I did not feel angry. The bodily contact of the crowd was a part of the reassurance that one was, and that one would be . . . that one was a part of the crowd . . . not a lonely crowd where each one fought for his own square foot to stand on, but a conglomerate crowd where the simple presence of other people held one up.

Wing Sung tapped Gordon's shoulder.

"We can go any time you like," he said. "My mother has dinner ready for us."

"Shouldn't we stay until the end of the program?"

"There are no rules about it . . . if you want to stand here until after midnight," he said lightly.

"I think I prefer your mother's cooking," Gordon answered.

"Where are the children?" I asked, shifting baby Christopher in my arms.

"They're backstage watching the actors put their make-up on, at least the girls are," Wing Sung said calmly.

"Oh no!"

"Never mind, Mei Ho took them backstage. One of the actors is our cousin."

"Where's Michael?"

"I think he might have gone on up to the house to help with the cooking. He's getting to be a good cook."

We found the girls, giggling and smeared with theatrical paint, out behind the platform. No one seemed to be upset about the fact, so we took it in stride.

I watched our two little girls . . . young daughters, they were becoming. Could it be almost four years since we had come back this time? Yes, when I looked at them, I could believe it. What a world of experiences they had had . . . we all had. They would hardly remember America when they went back for a visit. Would we? Was it possible to submerge oneself so thoroughly in a different culture that one's own ways became strange to him?

We wound our way up the hillside path, between small wooden structures and chicken yards. We stopped at a wooden gate, and Wing Sung called. Michael came and let us in, accompanied by Wong Tai, her round youthful face red from standing over the kerosene stove.

The frame living room was spotless, and the concrete floor

was tinted green. Calendar and magazine covers decorated the walls. In the center of the room stood a table, spread with endless varieties of Chinese food.

We sat around on folding chairs to eat, and I looked up. There were the household gods above us, in a large niche. A bronzed wooden goddess sat in her red surroundings, looking down over the room.

There was an uncomfortable pause. Wing Sung and his father exchanged glances. Wong SinSaang shifted his feet and said,

"Ding Mok-si, would you pray?"

Gordon did so, simply, in Chinese, and in Jesus' name.

We ate their food that night, and heard their jokes, and laughed into their eyes, and learned to play their games . . . and it was good.

It was dark and very late when we left the Wong home. Wing Sung went with us to help us find our way back past the maze of chicken yards and wooden houses to the main road. Gordon carried Christopher in a sleeping bundle in his arms, while the older children scampered ahead, proud of their sharp eyes in the dark. We had eaten and talked, and our spirits were high. We clambered down over the rocks, holding onto the sides of the houses, laughing from the sheer joy of the night and its sense of rightness.

There was the deep growl of a dog as we passed, and a voice inside a house . . .

"Those Westerners! Hear them laugh! They must be drunk. Old Wong Tai must have given them wine to drink."

Wing Sung heard the words too, and laughed.

"If wine can give men such happiness, why not God?" he said.

The words had a familiar ring, and I wondered if they were his own or if he were quoting them from his rich store of sayings. In his way, Wing Sung was coming to terms with himself and God, but he was too proud to take another's word for the way. His feet would have to find their own path, and his heart its own response, its own rhythm to bend with the wind . . . and it was good.

I paused and looked up at the sky. The blackness overhead, punctuated with pinpoints of light . . . How vast it was, and how unnumbered were the shapes and forms of light and dark that spread beneath it! I breathed in the cool night air and felt myself become a part of the sky, the expansiveness, the limitless life about me . . . the life and the sky and the air that were God's. How had I ever thought to win this world for God? It was His, long before I sprang into being, and long after I would be unremembered . . . And yet this brief span was not without meaning. Its meaning was to proclaim and live the love of God in every place at every time, under any circumstances . . . a living out of the meaning of love and reconciliation and acceptance . . . in honesty and without fear.

The hillside path crossed a narrow bridge and led into the road past the opera house. The music was still on, shrill and clear, accompanied by much clanging and banging of the cymbals and the beating of drums. The singer's voice floated out over the crowd, whining out human misery and joy while the people milled in and out of the building.

People were beginning to leave. The hour was late, and children were falling asleep. Soon the fishermen would have to go out to sea, and the market sellers would have to gather their early morning produce. They were passing us in the darkness now, going home. They nodded, and we said, "Rest early," and they replied, "Rest early." They were going home and we were going home, on the same street . . .

I looked out across the water. The sky and sea were one in the darkness, with only the lights of the fishing boats to show where the sea began. The whole pattern was light and darkness, vast areas of darkness with pinpoints of light . . . and everything was of a piece, a cohesion, a kindred substance.

Wing Sung walked quietly. I could not read his expression in the darkness, but he seemed meditative.

"Ding Mok-si," his voice broke the silence, "I wish my grandmother could have known you and Ding Tai."

Gordon shifted the sleeping baby in his arms.

"Your grandmother?" he asked.

"Yes. She died a few years ago. But I wish she had been at our house tonight so she could have met all of you. She hated people from the West."

"Why?"

"Ah, first she was old-fashioned, and felt that anyone who wasn't Chinese wasn't a human being . . . but I think there was something deeper than this. She felt that the foreigners only came here to take what they wanted and go."

"What made her feel this way?"

"Many things. I remember once when she became so angry at some foreigners . . . I was only a small boy then, but I remember it clearly . . . She always used it as an argument to prove why foreigners should be hated."

"What did they do?" I asked indignantly.

"One morning, when I was about twelve or so, a car came driving into the market and parked on the street across from my grandmother's stall. The man got out and went away, but the woman stayed in the car and began to draw a picture . . . a picture of my grandmother working, and a woman with a baby on her back. I was watching her, because I like to draw too, and I knew enough about these things to know that this woman could sell the picture for much money.

"When my grandmother found out what the woman was doing, she went over to her car and asked for a part of the money, since it was her likeness that was being drawn. But the woman refused. My Uncle Wong came over to the car to explain why the old lady was asking for money, and the woman locked the door in his face. Can you imagine such disrespect? My grandmother was so angry she went about muttering to herself for days . . . 'Those foreign devils, they have no manners . . . Steal an old woman's face to sell and not give her a penny . . .' "

I stopped walking, abruptly withdrawn from the expansiveness, the rightness. Gordon also stopped, and we stared at each other in the darkness. Wing Sung felt the charged air and spoke hurriedly.

"But now I know not everyone is that way," he said. "She

should have known you. Those were blackhearted Westerners . . .
not like you. I wish she had known you."

Gordon grasped my arm, and we resumed walking.

"Few people are blackhearted," Gordon said. "There are times
when we understand and times when we do not understand.
Misunderstanding acts like blackheartedness."

It was silent for a moment, with only the sound of our foot-
falls on the dirt road. The sea swished against the beach, and
the boat lights dipped and twinkled in the water. A street lamp
threw yellow highlights across our faces, and I glanced at Wing
Sung. His expression was one of puzzlement, of wondering what
he had said.

It was difficult to look at him. Of course he would not have
remembered us from that day long ago . . . We were only foreigners then, and they all looked alike to him. And how could
we have remembered him when to us he was only one of the
faceless four million a foreigner meets in Hong Kong? We had
met as kinds of people, not as human beings.

But dare we tell him now that the builders of the first bridges
he had known were also the stokers of his early fires of mistrust?
That the same human beings who had been invited to his table
tonight were those who had turned their backs on him once, in
ignorance and fear? That good and evil were not two men, but
in every man . . . in us?

I glanced again at his puzzled face, and knew. Yes, we dared.
We dared because we were not playing roles. We were not the
wise seeking to teach the foolish, the good seeking to eradicate
the bad. We were persons, capable of understanding and misunderstanding, of understanding a thousand things and failing to
understand a thousand more, and as persons we could dare to
share ourselves not only as we were but as we had been.

*The fences were down, and the lines were gone between us.
We were no longer foreigner and Chinese seeking to adapt and
bow to each other, dealing in bargains and tinged with mistrust.
We were a company of people walking along the road, surrounded by darkness but walking toward light . . . people with*

faces turned toward the wind . . . The Spring Wind, before which we must all bow as grass.

The night wind blew up from the sea, and we turned our faces toward home.